英 语 语 音 教 材

English Pronunciation for Chinese Speakers

© Linan Shi & Shasha Shi
The Key Publishing House Inc.

All rights reserved. No part of this publication may be reproduced, stored in a retrieval system, or transmitted, in any form or by any means, without prior written permission. Any person who does any unauthorized act in relation to this publication may be liable to criminal prosecution and civil claims for damages.

First Edition 2010
The Key Publishing House Inc.
Toronto, Canada
Website: www. thekeypublish. com
E-mail: info@thekeypublish. com
ISBN 978-0-9811606-5-8 paperback

Cover Design & Typesetting Alexa Jefferson
Proof reading and copyediting Jim Hanson

Library and Archives Canada Cataloguing in Publication

Shi, Linan
    English pronunciation for Chinese speakers / Linan Shi, Shasha Shi.

ISBN 978-0-9811606-5-8

    1. English language--Pronunciation by second language learners.
2. English language--Textbooks for second language learners--Chinese speakers. I. Shi, Shasha II. Title.

PE1137.S45 2010   428.2'4951   C2009-906434-0

Printed and bound in Canada. This book is printed on paper suitable for recycling and made from fully sustained forest sources.

Published by a grant and in association with The Key Research Center (www. thekeyresearch. org). The Key promotes freedom of thought and expression and peaceful coexistence among human societies.

石莎莎 和 石立男 合著

Authors

Linan Shi
&
Shasha Shi

加拿大多伦多市主流出版社
The Key Publishing House Inc.

作者前言

英语语音教材 是一本综合了英语发音理论与实践的全方位发音指南.

本书的编写充分地考虑到中国人发音的特点和习惯,结合了多年的教学经验并运用创新教学方法详细地讲解了北美的英文发音. 本书共有二十八课,每课课后都附有基于教学大纲和对学生评估后的实践练习,课文包括如何根据英语元音和辅音的发音,以及英语字母和字母组合的读音规则,来掌握英文单词和词组的发音方法.

作 者

二零零九年三月十六日

作者简介

石莎莎是加拿大多伦多市的一位英语教师，具有丰富的教授英语语音和英文基础的经验．在多年的教学过程中，她深刻了解到中国学生的语言特点和学习难处，积累了丰富的教学经验．石莎莎的启发式教学和循序渐进的训练方法深受学生们的推崇．本书的材料多取自于她的教学笔记．

石立男是加拿大多伦多市的英语教师，他还是加拿大国家翻译局的高级翻译，多伦多市教育局和安大略省社区多种语言翻译中心的翻译．石立男是《新英汉缩略语大辞典》的编委之一．石立男曾作为高级翻译陪同中国政府和企业领导及专业人员赴二十多个国家考察，谈判，引进设备等．他在移民加拿大前曾是中国某大学的英语助教，教授级高级翻译．他曾作为中国科技翻译家代表团的成员赴澳大利亚墨尔本参加"世界翻译家大会"，并在澳大利亚的"迪肯大学翻译研讨会"上宣读论文．他曾出席在澳大利亚悉尼大学召开的"世界比较教育大会"，并在大会的论文集上刊登了论文摘要．他曾在韩国首尔举办的"亚洲翻译家论坛"上宣读论文．他的翻译论文曾获得中国科技翻译论文一等奖．他的专业经历被登载在中国国家人事部出版的《中国高级专业人才大辞典》中．

Acknowledgements

This book would not have been possible without the support, dedication and immense work done by my family and for all their hard work, I offer my sincere gratitude to; my wife Guizhi Dong, my mother Xijun Chen, my father Lei Shi, my brother Yingnan Shi, my sister-in-law Shuqin Ma, my sister Lihua Shi, my brother-in-law Guozhang Wu, my niece Shanshan Shi and my nephew Jiashi Wu.

Linan Shi

感　　谢

在写此书的过程中,作者石立男的妻子 -- 董桂芝从各个方面对此书的编写做了大量的工作.
石立男的妈妈--陈锡钧,爸爸--石磊,弟弟--石英男,弟媳--麻淑琴,妹妹--石丽华,妹夫--吴国璋,侄女--石姗姗,外甥--吴家石也从各个方面对此书的编写做了大量的工作.在此,特向他们表示衷心地感谢!

作者:石立男

目　　录

第一课
- 1. 英语字母　　12
- 2. 英语字母书写笔划　　12
- 3. 英语字母的书写规格　　13

第二课
- 1. 元音字母辅音字母　　16
- 2. 英语字母表　　17

第三课
- 1. 元音音素和辅音音素　　19
- 2. 音标与国际音标　　23

第四课
- 1. 拼音　　27
- 2. 辅音音素 [p][b][t][d][k][g][j]　　28
- 3. 元音音素 [ei][əu][u:][i:][ai]　　31

第五课
- 1. 读音规则　　34
- 2. 音节　　34
- 3. 单音节词　　34
- 4. 重读音节的读音规则介绍　　34
- 5. 辅音音素 [f][v][s][z]　　35

第六课
- 1. 重读开音节　　38
- 2. 重读开音节的特殊情况　　38

第七课
- 1. 重读闭音节　　41
- 2. 元音音素[æ][ɔ][ʌ][e][i]　　42

第八课
- 1. 重读R音节　　45

	2. 重读R音节的特殊情况	46
	3. 元音音素: [ɑ:] [ɔ:] [ə:]	47
	4. 辅音音素: [h] [w] [r]	48
第九课		
	1. 重读开音节, 重读闭音节, 重读R音节的总结	49
第十课		
	1. 重读Re音节	52
	2. 定义	52
	3. 读音规则	52
	4. 元音音素: [ə][u][iə][ɛə] [uə]	53
第十一课		
	1. 部分辅音字母在单词中的读音	56
	2. 部分辅音字母组合在单词中的读音	56
	3. 辅音音素 [l] [m] [n] [ŋ]	57
第十二课		
	1. 辅音字母 Jj 在单词中的读音	61
	2. 部分辅音字母组合在单词中的读音	61
	3. 部分元音字母组合和元,辅音字母组合在单词中的读音	61
	4. 辅音音素 [θ] [ð] [ʃ] [ʒ] [tr] [dr] [ts] [dz] [tʃ] [dʒ]	62
	5. 元音音素 [au] [ɔi]	66
第十三课		
	1. 重读音节字母组合的介绍	68
	2. 重读音节字母组合的分类:	68
第十四课		
	1. 每个辅音字母在单词中的读音:	71
第十五课		
	1. 重读音节辅音字母组合在单词中的常用的读音规则:	74

第十六课		
	1. 重读音节元音字母组合在单词中的常用的读音规则：	77
	2. 重读音节元,辅音字母组合在单词中的常用的读音规则：	78

第十七课		
	1. 音节的划分	82
	2. 音节的划分规则	82
	3. 重读符号	82
	4. 三合元音	84

第十八课		
	1. 重读音节	89
	2. 非重读音节	89
	3. 元音字母在非重读音节中的规则的读音规则	89

第十九课		
	1. 元音字母在非重读音节中的不规则的读音规则	94
	2. 常用元,辅音字母组合在非重读音节中的读音规则	95
	3. 重读 Re 音节的特殊情况	96

第二十课		
	1. 常用的音变现象	98

第二十一课		
	1. S _ 辅音连缀	101
	2. 浊化	103

第二十二课		105
	1. 常用的连读现象	

第二十三课		107
	1. 爆破音	

第二十四课		109
	1. 实词和功能词的读音规则	

| 第二十五课 | | 111 |

	1.	停顿	
	2.	意群	
第二十六课			
	1.	英语的节奏	113
第二十七课			
	1.	语调: 升调	115
第二十八课			
	1.	语调: 降调	119

常用英语语音表格

1. 英语元音音素发音说明   124
2. 英语辅音音素发音说明   131
3. 英语音素发音说明   143
4. 元音音素的常用读音规则练习表   161
5. 元音音素的常用读音规则练习表（附带说明）   171
6. 辅音音素的常用读音规则练习表   181
7. 辅音音素的常用读音规则练习表（附带说明）   192
8. 英语拼音表（辅音拼元音）   203
9. 英语拼音表（辅音拼元音）(特殊情况的说明)   206
10. 英语拼音练习表（辅音拼元音）   207
11. 英语拼音练习表（辅音拼元音）(特殊情况的说明)   211
12. 英语元音字母的常用读音规则表   212
13. 英语辅音字母的常用读音规则表   213
14. 英语 26 个字母的常用读音规则表   215
15. 英语元音字母或字母组合的常用读音规则表   218
16. 英语元音字母或字母组合的读音规则表（特殊情况的说明）   224
17. 英语辅音字母或字母组合的常用读音规则表   226
18. 英语辅音字母或字母组合的读音规则表（特殊情况的说明）   231
19. 英语字母或字母组合的常用读音规则表   232
20. 英语字母或字母组合的常用读音规则表（特殊情况的说明）   243

English Pronunciation for Chinese Speakers

语音教材

第一课　　　英语字母

英 语 字 母	英语是拼音文字,每个英语单词都是由英语字母表中的 26 个字母构成的. 例如 English (英语), 就是由 e, n, g, l, i, s, h 这七个字母构成的.
	英语字母是书写英语单词的最小单位, 每个英语字母都自其各自的大写体和小写体.
	英语句子的第一个字母必须大写, 句末必须有标点符号, 例如: English is an art (英语是一门艺术).
	在表达专有名词的人名, 地名时, 此单词的第一个字母必须大写, 例如: Toronto 多伦多　John 约翰.

英语字母书写笔划如下：（大写）

英语字母书写笔划如下:（小写）

英语字母的书写规格顺口溜	
三个格来四条线，	流利书写是门面．
大写字母上中格，	不要顶着第一线．
小写字母细分辨，	掌握规律慢慢练．
字母 b d h k l，	上端顶着第一线．
t 的上端 i 的点，	都在第一格中间．
小写字母 t 和 f，	横划紧贴第二线．
小写字母 f j p，	上端都在一格间．
f g j p q 和 y，	下端都抵第四线．

English Pronunciation for Chinese Speakers

第一课   练习
Lesson One   Exercises

1. 跟老师读26个英语字母 (大写字母)

A	B	C	D	E	F	G	H	I	J	K	L	M
N	O	P	Q	R	S	T	U	V	W	X	Y	Z

2. 朗读下面表示人名，地名的专有名词 (大写字母)

TORONTO	CANADA
ONTARIO	OTTOWA
BEIJING	CHINA
SHANGHAI	TIANJIN
MARTIN	JOHN
ELIZABETH	MARGARET

3. 听写英语字母 (大写字母)

U. S. A.	WASHINGTON
BRITISH	LONDON
FRANCE	PARIS
GERMANY	BERLIN
ITALY	ROME
JAPAN	TOKYO

4. 抄写26个英语字母（大写字母）

5. 跟老师读 26 个英语字母 (小写字母)												
a	b	c	d	e	f	g	h	i	j	k	l	m
n	o	p	q	r	s	t	u	v	w	x	y	z

6. 朗读下面小写字母	
c e n t	d o l l a r
c o i n	b i l l
m a p l e	l e a f
b e a v e r	s c h o o n e r
c a r i b o u	l o o n
n o r t h	p o l a r
b e a r	m o n e y

7. 听写英语字母 (小写字母)	
a b d p q	c e i m n o r
s u v w x z	b d f h k l
g j p q y	a b d q y
f g p q y	e i j l t y

8. 抄写 26 个英语字母 （小写字母）

第二课　　　　元音字母和辅音字母

元音字母	元音字母共有6个，它们是构成英语单词的最基本要素. 任何一个英语单词中，至少有一个元音字母. 一定要把元音字母记熟，读准. A a, O o, U u, E e, I i, Y y. (有观点认为英语有5个元音字母，y是半元音字母，这种说法也是正确的. 因为y既可以作元音字母,也可作辅音字母.)
辅音字母	辅音字母的功能是帮助元音字母构成一个完整的英语单词的，例如: good. 辅音字母g和d 都是帮助元音字母 o o 构成 good 这个单词，而缺乏元音字母的g 和d 在一起不能构成英语单词. 辅音字母是二十六个字母中除去元音字母外剩余的二十个.（说明: y 如果在元音字母前，它是辅音字母. y 作辅音字母时只能发 [j] 音，和后边的元音相拼，例如: yes [jes].)

发音有相同音的英语字母	
元 音 字 母	辅 音 字 母
A a	H h　　J j　　　　K k
O o	
U u	Q q　　W w
E e	B b　C c　D d　G g　P p　T t　V v
I i (Y y)	Y y
	R r
	F f　L l　M m　N n　S s　X x　Z z

英语字母表								
印刷体		手写体		发音	印刷体		手写体		发音
大写	小写	大写	小写		大写	小写	大写	小写	
A	a	A	a	[ei]	N	n	N	n	[en]
B	b	B	b	[bi:]	O	o	O	o	[əu]
C	c	C	c	[si:]	P	p	P	p	[pi:]
D	d	D	d	[di:]	Q	q	Q	q	[kju:]
E	e	E	e	[i:]	R	r	R	r	[ɑ:]
F	f	F	f	[ef]	S	s	S	s	[es]
G	g	G	g	[dʒi:]	T	t	T	t	[ti:]
H	h	H	h	[eitʃ]	U	u	U	u	[ju:]
I	i	I	i	[ai]	V	v	V	v	[vi:]
J	j	J	j	[dʒei]	W	w	W	w	[ˈdʌblju:]
K	k	K	k	[kei]	X	x	X	x	[eks]
L	l	L	l	[el]	Y	y	Y	y	[wai]
M	m	M	m	[em]	Z	z	Z	z	[zed]

第二课   练习
Lesson Two   Exercises

1. 朗读下列大写字母					
U V W	D O Q	L S Z	B E F	M N W
H N U	B G R	C D G	I L Y	A K R

2. 朗读下列小写字母				
a b d	h m n	p q g	a c e	i j l
f I t	s x z	k r y	u v w	o p q

3. 填写对应的大写字母或小写字母						
A___	C___	E___	G___	I___	K___	L___ N___
O___	Q___	S___	U___	V___	W___	X___ Y___
b___	d___	f___	h___	j___	l___	n___ p___
r___	t___	v___	x___	z___		

第三课　　　　音素 音标 国际音标

音素	英语中,音素是语音的最小单位. 英语字母表的 26 个字母所发出的４８个音就是音素. 这４８个音素, 也就是４８个音标. 音素分为元音音素和辅音音素,元音音素简称为元音,辅音音素简称为辅音. 请注意: 切忌把元音音素和元音字母混淆,也避免把辅音音素和辅音字母混淆.
长元音	有 ":" 符号的元音叫长元音. 在发音时, 发音时间要比其它元音长.（长一拍）
短元音	没有 ":" 符号的元音叫短元音. 在发音时, 发音时间要短, 不能长.
单元音	单词中只有一个元音的音素叫单元音. 单元音包括 5 个长元音和 7 个短元音. 共有 12 个单元音.
双元音	单词中有两个元音的音素是双元音. 共有 8 个双元音.
双元音的特点	第一个元音长而清楚, 第二个元音短而模糊. 发音时, 由第一个元音滑向第二个元音.

发　音　特　点	
元音音素	元音音素: 发音时声带振动,气流通过口腔时,不受舌,颚,齿, 唇等发音器官的阻碍. 元音音素共有二十个.
辅音音素	辅音音素: 发音时,气流通过口腔时,一律受到舌,颚,齿,唇等发音器官的阻碍. 辅音音素共有二十八个. 辅音音素分清辅音和浊辅音两种.
清辅音	发音时, 声带不振动. 共有十一个清辅音.
浊辅音	发音时, 声带振动. 共有十七个浊辅音.

音素表：（1）

二十个元音表						
单元音	前元音	[i:]	[i]	[e]	[æ]	
	中元音	[ʌ]	[ə]	[ə:]		
	后元音	[ɑ:]	[ɔ]	[ɔ:]	[u]	[u:]
双元音	合口双元音	[ei]	[ai]	[au]	[əu]	[ɔi]
	开口双元音	[iə]	[ɛə]	[uə]		

音素表：（2）

二十个元音表							
单元音	长元音	[i:]	[ə:]	[ɑ:]	[ɔ:]	[u:]	
	短元音	[i]	[e]	[æ]	[ʌ]	[ə]	[ɔ]	[u]
双元音	合口双元音	[ei]	[ai]	[au]	[əu]	[ɔi]	
	开口双元音	[iə]	[ɛə]	[uə]			

音素表:（3）

二 十 八 个 辅 音 表						
爆破音	[p]	[b]	[t]	[d]	[k]	[g]
唇齿摩擦音	[f]	[v]				
舌齿摩擦音	[s]	[z]	[θ]	[ð]		
软颚摩擦音	[ʃ]	[ʒ]				
破擦音	[ts]	[dz]	[tr]	[dr]	[tʃ]	[dʒ]
声门摩擦音	[h]					
摩擦音	[j]	[w]	[r]			
摩擦音	[l]					
鼻音	[m]	[n]	[ŋ]			

音素表:（4）

十 对 清, 浊 辅 音	
清辅音	浊辅音
[p]	[b]
[t]	[d]
[k]	[g]
[f]	[v]
[s]	[z]
[θ]	[ð]
[ʃ]	[ʒ]
[ts]	[dz]
[tr]	[dr]
[tʃ]	[dʒ]

音素表:（5）

不 成 对 清, 浊 辅 音	
清辅音	浊辅音
[h]	[j]
	[w]
	[r]
	[l]
	[m]
	[n]
	[ŋ]

音 标	
音标	是英语单词的注音符号或叫英语单词的标音符号，一个音标代表一个音素.
英语单词中的同一个字母(或字母组合)可以有不同的读音，而不同的字母 (或字母组合) 也可以有相同的读音. 例如:	
1.	英语字母 A a : (aim, bake, hat, lark, ago) 同是英语字母 A a, 发音却不同. Same letter, different sound, 即: 所谓的 "字同音不同".
2.	英语字母组合 (ei, ey, ay, ai, veil, they, say, saint) 这些不同的字母组合却有相同的读音. Same sound, different letters, 即: 所谓的 "音同字不同". 所以, 不能用原来字母表示所有的音.
3.	要准确地读出一个英语单词，就需要有一套英语单词的注音符号，这套英语单词的注音符号就是音标. 对于把英语作为第二语言的中国学生，要想学好英语,必须先打好两个基本功: 语音和语法, 再掌握听, 说, 读, 写, 译 5 个技巧.因此, 学习语音,就得先学好音标.

国际音标	International Phonetic Alphabet, 简称 IPA. 国际音标共有 48 个. 因为大多数国际音标与英语小写字母的形状相同, 为了避免混淆, 国际音标都放在 [ ] 内.

国 际 音 标 表				
元 音 音 素		例	词	
前元音	[i:]	beat	[bi:t]	节拍
	[I]	sit	[sit]	坐
	[e]	desk	[desk]	书桌
	[æ]	bad	[bæd]	坏的
中元音	[ʌ]	but	[bʌt]	但是
	[ə]	ago	[əˈgəu]	以前
	[ə:]	first	[fə:st]	第一
后元音	[ɑ:]	art	[ɑ:t]	艺术

	[ɔ]	not	[nɔt]	不
	[ɔ:]	fork	[fɔ:k]	叉子
	[u]	book	[buk]	书
	[u:]	blue	[blu:]	蓝色的
合口双元音	[e i]	bake	[beik]	烘烤
	[a i]	bike	[baik]	自行车
	[a u]	now	[nau]	现在
	[ə u]	no	[nəu]	不
	[ɔ i]	boy	[bɔi]	男孩
开口双元音	[iə]	hear	[hiə]	听到
	[εə]	hair	[hεə]	头发
	[uə]	tour	[tuə]	旅行

国 际 音 标 表					
辅 音 音 素		清, 浊辅音		例 词	
双唇爆破音	[p]	清		place	[pleis]	地方
	[b]		浊	bike	[baik]	自行车
舌前-齿龈爆破音	[t]	清		time	[taim]	时间
	[d]		浊	date	[deit]	日期
舌后-软颚 爆破音	[k]	清		kite	[kait]	风筝
	[g]		浊	game	[geim]	游戏
下唇-上齿摩擦音	[f]	清		five	[faiv]	五
	[v]		浊	vote	[vəut]	选举
舌前-下齿摩擦音	[s]	清		save	[seiv]	储蓄
	[z]		浊	zone	[zəun]	地区
舌前-上齿外摩擦音	[θ]	清		third	[θə:d]	第三
	[ð]		浊	this	[ðis]	这
舌前-硬颚摩擦音	[ʃ]	清		short	[ʃɔ:t]	短的

		[ʒ]		浊	beige	[beiʒ]	米色
破擦音 (既有爆破音又有摩擦音)		[ts]	清		pets	[pets]	宠物
		[dz]		浊	beds	[bedz]	床
		[tr]	清		tree	[tri:]	树
		[dr]		浊	dry	[drai]	干的
		[tʃ]	清		cheap	[tʃi:p]	便宜的
		[dʒ]		浊	jeep	[dʒi:p]	吉普车
声门摩擦音		[h]	清		help	[help]	帮助
舌前-硬颚摩擦音		[j]		浊	yes	[jes]	是的
舌中-硬颚摩擦音		[r]		浊	red	[red]	红色的
舌后-软颚摩擦音		[w]		浊	wet	[wet]	湿的
舌侧音 (或旁流音)		[l]		浊	let	[let]	让
				浊	glad	[glæd]	高兴
		[l]		浊	bill	[bil]	纸币
				浊	milk	[milk]	牛奶
双唇-鼻音		[m]		浊	map	[mæp]	地图
舌前-齿龈鼻音		[n]		浊	name	[neim]	名字
舌后-软颚鼻音		[ŋ]		浊	long	[lɔŋ]	长的

第三课　　　练习
Lesson Three　　Exercises

1.	字母和音素的区别	
2.	音标的定义是什么	
3.	什么是国际音标	

第四课

拼音	英语是拼音文字，但是它的拼音规则和中文的拼音规则很相似. 中文是声母拼韵母，声母就似辅音，韵母就似元音.英语是辅音拼元音. 注意，辅音不能拼辅音，元音不能拼元音；元音不能拼辅音，只有辅音才能拼元音.

元音字母的读音	
元音字母	读音
A a	[e i]
O o	[ə u]
U u	[j u:]
E e	[i:]
I i (Y y)	[a i]

某些辅音字母的读音	
辅音字母	读音
P p	[p]
B b	[b]
T t	[t]
D d	[d]
K k	[k]
G g	[g]

辅音字母 p, b, t, d, k, g 拼元音字母 a, o, u, e, i, y 的拼音表					
元音字母 \ 辅音字母	Aa [e i]	Oo [ə u]	Uu [j u:]	Ee [i:]	Ii(Yy)[a i]
P [p]	p a	po	pu	pe	pi
B [b]	b a	bo	bu	be	bi
T [t]	t a		tu	te	ti
D [d]	d a		du	de	di
K [k]	k a	ko	ku	ke	ki
G [g]	g a	go			

辅音音素 [p] [b] [t] [d] [k] [g] [j]

[p] 双唇爆破音	
[p] 和 [b] 是一对清,浊辅音. [p] 发音时, 双唇紧闭, 憋住一口气, 不能卷舌, 要平伸于口中, 不能碰到上齿和下齿, 然后让气流从口腔中突然冲开双唇的阻碍, 爆破成音. 发音时, 口腔部位与发 [b] 和 [m] 音的口腔部位相同. [p] 音与普通话中的"坡"的声母音相似, 但不相同, 需要去掉"坡"的声母音的尾音, 还要有爆破, 才能发出 [p] 音. 发音结束时, 口型是扁的, 张开的, 不要闭上嘴. 它是清辅音.	
发音三要素	1. 唇势: 双唇紧闭　　2. 齿距: 几乎闭合 3. 舌位: 平伸于口中

[b] 双唇爆破音	
[p] 和 [b] 是一对清,浊辅音.发音时, 双唇紧闭, 憋住一口气, 不能卷舌, 要平伸于口中, 不能碰到上齿和下齿, 然后让气流从口腔中突然冲开双唇的阻碍, 爆破成音.发音时,口腔部位与发 [p] 和 [m] 音的口腔部位相同. [b] 音与普通话中的"玻"的声母音相似, 但不相同, 需要去掉"玻"的声母音的尾音, 还要有爆破, 才能发出[b]音.发音结束时,口型是扁的, 张开的, 不要闭上嘴.它是浊辅音.	
发音三要素	1. 唇势: 双唇紧闭　　2. 齿距: 几乎闭合 3. 舌位: 平伸于口中

[t] 舌前 - 齿龈爆破音
[t] 和 [d] 是一对清,浊辅音. [t] 发音时,舌尖抵紧上齿龈,憋住一口气, 形成阻力, 然后让气流从口腔中舌尖和齿龈间突然冲出, 爆破成音.发音时, 口腔部位与发 [d], [l] 和 [n] 音的口腔部位相同. [t] 音与普通话中的 "脱"的声母音相似, 但不相同.需要去掉"脱"的声母音的尾音, 还要有爆破,才能发出 [t] 音.发音结束时,口型是扁的,张开的,不要闭上嘴.它是清辅音.

发音三要素	1. 唇势: 扁　　　　2. 齿距: 几乎闭合
	3. 舌位: 舌尖抵紧上齿龈

[d] 舌前 - 齿龈爆破音	
[t] 和 [d] 是一对清,浊辅音. [d] 发音时, 舌尖抵紧上齿龈, 憋住一口气, 形成阻力, 然后让气流从口腔中的舌尖和齿龈间突然冲出, 爆破成音.发音时, 口腔部位与发 [t], [l] 和 [n] 音的口腔部位相同. [d] 音与普通话中的"的"的声母音相似, 但不相同.得去掉"的"的声母音的尾音, 还要有爆破, 才能发出 [d] 音.发音结束时, 口型是扁的, 张开的, 不要闭上嘴. 它是浊辅音.	
发音三要素	1. 唇势: 扁　　　　2. 齿距: 几乎闭合
	3. 舌位: 舌尖抵紧上齿龈

[k] 舌后 - 软颚爆破音	
发音时,舌跟贴近软颚,憋住一口气,形成阻力,然后让气流从口腔中的舌跟和软颚间突然冲出,爆破成音.发音时, 口腔部位与发 [g] 和 [ŋ] 音的口腔部位相同 [k] 音与普通话中的"科"的声母音相似,但不相同.要去掉"科"的声母音的尾音,还要有爆破,才能发出 [k] 音发音结束时, 口型是扁的, 张开的, 不要闭上嘴. 它是清辅音. [k] 和 [g] 是一对清,浊辅音.	
发音三要素	1. 唇势: 扁　　　　2. 齿距: 半个扁指
	3. 舌位: 舌跟贴近软颚

[g] 舌后 - 软颚爆破音
发音时,舌跟贴近软颚,憋住一口气,形成阻力,然后让气流从口腔中的舌跟和软颚间突然冲出, 爆破成音. 发音时, 口腔部位与发 [k] 和 [ŋ] 音的口腔部位相同. [g] 音与普通话中的"哥"的声母音相似, 但不相同.要去掉"哥"的声母音的尾音, 还要有爆破, 才能发出 [g] 音. 发音结束时, 口型是扁的, 张开的, 不要闭上嘴. 它是浊辅音. [k] 和 [g] 是一对清,浊辅音.

发音三要素	1. 唇势: 扁　　　　2. 齿距: 半个扁指
	3. 舌位: 舌跟贴近软颚

[j] 舌前 - 硬颚摩擦音	
发音时, 舌前和硬颚间要有空隙, 此时, 憋住一口气, 形成阻力, 舌尖抵下齿.嘴唇是扁的, 上下牙齿几乎闭合, 然后让气流从舌前和硬颚间冲出, 摩擦成音. [j] 音与普通话中的"耶"的声母音相似, 但不相同. 要去掉"耶"的声母音的尾音, 还要让气流从舌前和硬颚间冲出, 摩擦成 [j] 音. 发音结束时, 可以松口气, 但是要保持发音时的口型, 不要闭嘴. 它是浊辅音.	
发音三要素	1. 唇势: 扁　　　　2. 齿距: 几乎闭合
	3. 舌位: 舌尖抵下齿

元音音素 [ei] [əu] [u:] [i:] [ai]

[ei] 合口双元音	
合口双元音 [ei] 是由第一个元音 [e] 向第二个元音 [i] 滑动发音时，嘴型一定要从大到小滑动. [ei] 音与普通话拼音中的"ei"音相似，但不相同. 普通话拼音中的"ei"音太放松, 嘴型大, 且没有滑动. 而发合口双元音 [ei] 音时, 由第一个元音 [e] 向第二个元音 [i] 滑动, 嘴型一定要从大到小滑动, 才能发出合口双元音 [ei] 音. 发音结束时, 舌尖仍然抵下牙齿, 不要闭嘴.	
发音三要素	1. 唇势: 扁 2. 齿距: 从一个扁指滑动到半个扁指 3. 舌位: 舌前部紧抵下齿

[əu] 合口双元音	
合口双元音 [əu] 是由第一个元音 [ə] 向第二个元音 [u] 滑动发音时, 嘴型一定要从大到小滑动. [əu] 音与普通话拼音中的"沤"音相似, 但不相同. 普通话拼音中的"沤"音只有一个音, 而发合口双元音 [əu] 音时, 要由第一个元音 [ə] 向第二个元音 [u] 音滑动, 嘴型一定要从大到小滑动, 才能发出合口双元音 [əu] 音. 发音结束时, 嘴型是小圆.	
发音三要素	1. 唇势: 嘴型从扁到小圆 2. 齿距: 从两个扁指滑动到一个半个扁指 3.舌位: 发音时, 从舌中部滑动到舌后部上抬拢音. 以唇势: 小圆, 齿距: 一个半个扁指, 舌位: 舌后部上抬拢音结束发音.

[u:] 后元音
后元音, 即舌后部（舌根）活动. [u:] 音与普通话中的"务"音相似, 但不相同.普通话中的"务"音太放松, 而发后元音 [u:] 音时, 口是小圆形. 舌头平伸于口中, 舌前部和舌中部都不要碰到上齿和下齿.发音时, 舌后部要上抬, 尽量要向里拢音. [u:] 是长元音. 发音结束时, 仍然保持原来的口型, 不要闭嘴.

发音三要素	1. 唇势: 口是小圆形　　　2. 齿距: 一个半扁指
	3. 舌位: 舌头平伸于口中. 舌前部和舌中部都不要碰到上齿和下齿, 发音时舌后部上抬.

[i:] 前元音

前元音, 即舌前部（舌尖）活动. [i:] 音与普通话中的"一"音相似, 但不相同. 发前元音 [i:] 音时, 音要发得长点因为有长音符号, [i:] 是长元音. 发音结束时, 舌尖仍然抵住下牙齿.

发音三要素	1. 唇势: 最扁　　　2. 齿距: 几乎闭合
	3. 舌位: 舌尖抵紧下牙齿

[ai] 合口双元音

合口双元音 [ai] 是由第一个元音 [a] 向第二个元音 [i] 滑动发音时, 嘴型一定要从大到小滑动. [ai] 音与普通话拼音中的"啊"和合口双元音 [ei] 的第二个元音 [i] 的发音相似, 但不相同. 普通话拼音中的"啊"音太放松, 而发合口双元音中的 [a] 音时, 口全开, 舌下压. 因此, 发合口双元音 [ai] 音时, 要由第一个元音 [a] 向第二个元音 [i] 滑动, 嘴型一定要从大到小滑动, 才能发出合口双元音 [ai] 音. 发音结束时, 舌尖仍然抵下牙齿, 不要闭嘴.

发音三要素	1. 唇势: 嘴型从口全开滑动到很扁
	2. 齿距: 从三个扁指滑动到半个扁指
	3. 舌位: 从舌后部活动滑动到舌前部, 发音后, 以舌尖紧抵下牙齿结束发音.

第四课　　　　　练习
Lesson Four　　Exercises

辅音音素和元音音素的拼读练习					
元音＼辅音	[e i]	[ə u]	[j u:]	[i:]	[ai]
[p]	[p e i]	[p ə u]	[p j u:]	[p i:]	[p a i]
[b]	[b e i]	[b ə u]	[b j u:]	[b i:]	[b a i]
[t]	[t e i]	[t ə u]	[t j u:]	[t i:]	[t a i]
[d]	[d e i]	[d ə u]	[d j u:]	[d i:]	[d a i]
[k]	[k e i]	[k ə u]	[k j u:]	[k i:]	[k a i]
[g]	[g e i]	[g ə u]	[g j u:]	[g i:]	[g a i]

第五课

读音规则	虽然英语单词的读音千变万化，但也有规律可循。我们按单词的拼写形式去读英语字母音的规则，就是读音规则。
音节	音节是说话时最小的语言片断。含有一个响亮音素的声音片断，就是一个音节。英语里的元音音素都是响亮的音素，所以都是音节。一个元音音素就是一个音节，有几个元音音素就有几个音节，但不是元音字母。单独一个元音字母也能构成一个音节。例如：I [ai] 等。辅音就不能构成音节，但辅音 [l m n] 在词尾时，可以和它前面的辅音构成成音节，都是非重读音节，例如：little [ˈlitl]（""是重读符号）。
单音节词	只有一个音节的词。单音节词都是重读音节，但重读符号全部省略。
重读音节共有五种读音规则	1. 重读开音节 2. 重读闭音节 3. 重读 R 音节 4. 重读 Re 音节 5. 重读字母组合

某些辅音字母的读音：

辅 音 字 母	读 音
F f	[f]
V v	[v]
S s	[s]
Z z	[z]

辅音字母 f, v, s, z 拼元音字母 a, o, u, e, i, y 音的拼音表					
元音字母 辅音字母	Aa [e i]	Oo [ə u]	Uu [j u:]	Ee [i:]	Ii(Yy)[a i]
f [f]	fa	fo	fu	fe	fi
v [v]	va	vo		ve	vi
s [s]	sa	so	su	se	si
z [z]	za	zo		ze	zi

辅音音素 [f] [v] [s] [z]

[f] 下唇 - 上齿摩擦音		
[f] 和 [v] 是一对清,浊辅音. [f] 发音时,上齿咬住下唇,憋住一口气,形成阻力,然后让气流从上齿和下唇间冲出,摩擦成音. 发音时,口腔部位与发 [v] 音的口腔部位相同. [f] 音与普通话中的"夫"的声母音相似,但不相同. 得去掉"夫"的声母音的尾音,还要让你的下唇和上齿摩擦,才能发出 [f] 音发音结束时,上齿仍然咬住下唇,不要松开. 它是清辅音.		
发音三要素	1. 唇势: 扁　　　2. 齿距: 下唇的厚度 3. 舌位: 上齿咬住下唇,舌平伸于口中	

[v] 下唇 - 上齿摩擦音		
[f] 和 [v] 是一对清,浊辅音. [v] 发音时,上齿咬住下唇,憋住一口气,形成阻力,然后让气流从上齿和下唇间冲出,摩擦成音. 发音时,口腔部位与发 [f] 音的口腔部位相同. 普通话中没有 [v] 音,可用上齿咬住下唇,憋住一口气,形成阻力,然后让气流从上齿和下唇间摩擦成"屋"音. 发音结束时,上齿仍然咬住下唇,不要松开. 它是浊辅音.		
发音三要素	1. 唇势: 扁　　　2. 齿距: 下唇的厚度 3. 舌位: 上齿咬住下唇,舌平伸于口中	

[s] 舌前 - 下齿摩擦音		
[s] 和 [z] 是一对清,浊辅音. [s] 发音时,舌尖抵紧下齿,憋住一口气,形成阻力,然后让气流从舌尖和下齿间冲出,摩擦成音. 发音时,口腔部位与发[z]音的口腔部位相同. [s] 音 与普通话拼音中的"s"音相似,但不相同.发音时,要用舌前和下齿摩擦发出 [s] 音. 注意: 舌前和下齿摩擦发出 [s] 音比舌前和上齿摩擦发出 [s] 音更容易,更准确. 发音结束时,舌尖仍然抵下齿,舌尖不要离开下齿. 它是清辅音.		
发音三要素	1. 唇势: 扁　　　2. 齿距: 闭合 3. 舌位: 舌尖抵紧下齿	

[z] 舌前 - 下齿摩擦音	
[s] 和 [z] 是一对清、浊辅音. [z] 发音时，舌尖抵紧下齿，憋住一口气，形成阻力，然后让气流从舌尖和下齿间冲出，摩擦成音. 发音时，口腔部位与发 [s] 音的口腔部位相同. 普通话中没有 [z] 音，可以用舌尖抵下齿，憋住一口气，形成阻力，然后让气流从舌尖和下齿间摩擦成一个相似于普通话拼音中的 "r" 音. 但是，这与普通话拼音中的 "r" 音不相同. 普通话拼音中的 "r" 音是卷舌音，而国际音标 [z] 却不能卷舌（国际音标中没有卷舌音. 发音时，要用舌前和下齿摩擦才能发出 [z] 音. 发音要领是舌前和下齿摩擦发出 [s] 音. 比舌前和上齿摩擦发出 [s] 音更容易，更准确. 发音结束时，舌尖仍然抵下齿，舌尖不要离开下齿. 它是浊辅音.	
发音三要素	1. 唇势: 扁　　　　2. 齿距: 闭合 3. 舌位: 舌尖抵紧下齿

第五课　　　　　练习
Lesson Five　　Exercises

1. 问: 什么是读音规则?	答:
2. 问: 什么是音节?	答:

3. 辅音音素和元音音素的拼读练习:

辅音＼元音	[e i]	[ə u]	[j u:]	[i:]	[ai]
[f]	[f e i]	[f ə u]	[f j u:]	[f i:]	[f a i]
[v]	[v e i]	[v ə u]	[v j u:]	[v i:]	[v a i]
[s]	[s e i]	[s ə u]	[s j u:]	[s i:]	[s a i]
[z]	[z e i]	[z ə u]		[z i:]	[z a i]

第六课 重读开音节

定义	以一个元音字母结尾的音节叫开音节 (在单音节词中).
读音规则	元音字母在重读开音节中读其字母的名称音. a 读 [e i]　　　o 读 [ə u] u 读 [j u:]　　　Ee 读 [i:] Ii (Yy) 读 [a i]

元音字母 / 辅音字母	Aa [e i]	Oo [ə u]	Uu [j u:]	Ee [i:]	Ii(Yy) [a i]
p [p]	pa	po	pu	pe	pi
b [b]	ba	bo	bu	be	bi

为什么叫开音节	因为在开音节中, 元音字母后什么也没有. 例如: be 元音字母 "e" 后什么也没有. 换句话说: 没有任何东西把元音字母 "e" 关闭起来. 元音字母"e"是敞开的, 所以, 叫开音节.

重 读 开 音 节 的 特 殊 情 况

定义	以一个元音字母 + 一个辅音字母 + 一个不发音的 e 结尾的音节叫开 音节的特殊情况 (在单音节词中).
读音规则	元音字母在重读开音节的特殊情况中读其字母的名称音.

元音字母 / 辅音字母	Aa [e i]	Oo [ə u]	Uu [j u:]	Ee [i:]	Ii(Yy) [a i]
p [p]	pate	poke	puke	peke	pike
b [b]	bade	bode	bute	Bede	bike
t [t]	take	tote	tube	tene	tide
d [d]	date	dose	dude	deke	dive

		读 熟, 读 准 六 个 元 音 字 母
Aa	[e i]	Kate and Lake say: bake, cake, date, gate, pave, face and save.
Oo	[ə u]	Note the Note "No Smoking !"
Uu	[j u:]	A few new users and a few new students use a few new tubes with you.
Ee	[i:]	Lee, Dee and Kee see bee.
Ii	[a i]	I ride my white, light bike at night.
Yy	[w a i]	Why does Ryan type many types of white bikes?

English Pronunciation for Chinese Speakers

第六课 练习
Lesson Six Exercises

1.	什么叫开音节	
2.	开音节的读音规则是什么	
3.	开音节特殊情况的定义是什么	
4.	开音节特殊情况的读音规则是什么	

5. 开音节的拼读练习						
[e i]	[e i p]	[e i t]	[t e i k]	[d e i t]	[p e i]	[s e i]
[ə u]	[ə u d]	[ə u k]	[b ə u d]	[pə u d]	[b ə u]	[f ə u]
[j u:]	[j u: s]	[j u: k]	[t j u:b]	[p j u:k]	[f j u:]	[v j u:]
[i:]	[i:v]	[i: t]	[s i: d]	[p i: k]	[k i:]	[b i:]
[a i]	[a i]	[a i s]	[t a i p]	[k a i t]	[s k a i]	[s p a i]

6. 朗读下列单词并写出音标				
bake	Pope	duke	eve	type
bye	peke	tube	dose	tape
be	tide	dude	poke	pate
go	ape	by	cede	I

第七课　　重读闭音节

定义	以一个元音字母 + 一个或几个辅音字母 (r 除外) 结尾的音节叫重读闭音节 (在单音节词中).
读音规则	元音字母在闭音节中读其规定的短元音. 即: Aa 读　　　[æ]　　Oo 读　　　[ɔ] Uu 读　　　[ʌ]　　Ee 读　　　[e] Ii { Yy } 读　　[i]

元音字母 / 辅音字母	Aa [æ]	Oo [ɔ]	Uu [ʌ]	Ee [e]	Ii(Yy) [i]
p [p]	pap	Pop	pub	pep	pip
b [b]	bag	Bog	bug	beg	big
t [t]	tap	top	tup	ted	tip
d [d]	dab	Dob	dub	deb	dib

读熟,读准五个短元音音素	
Aa　　　[æ]	Pack, Sam and Matt had a sad Saturday.
Oo　　　[ɔ]	Bob, Mock, and Tom are not in the dock.
Uu　　　[ʌ]	Dud and Tuff are in such hurry.
Ee　　　[e]	Peg, Ned, Helen, Sell, and Ted fed ten pets at ten ten.
Ii (Yy) [i]	Bill, Dick, Fist, Hill, Kidd, Lily Nick, Rick will dig a big pit.

为什么叫闭音节	因为在闭音节中,一个元音字母后跟一个或几个辅音字母结尾. 换句话说: 这个元音字母被一个或几个辅音字母关闭起来了. 例如: 在单词 "tap" 中, 元音字母 "a" 后跟一个辅音字母 "p". 换句话说: 这个元音字母 "a" 被辅音字母 "p" 关闭起来了. 在单词 "best" 中, 元音字母 "e" 后跟两个辅音字母 "st". 换句话说: 这个元音字母 "e" 被两个辅音字母 "st" 关闭起来了.

元音音素 [æ] [ɔ] [ʌ] [e] [i]

[æ] 前元音
前元音, 即舌前部活动. 舌前部就是舌尖. [æ] 音与普通话中的 "碍" 音相似, 但不相同. 普通话中的 "碍" 音太长, 而前元音 [æ] 音是短元音. 在发音结束时, 舌尖仍然抵住下牙齿.

发音三要素	1. 唇势: 扁　　　　　2. 齿距: 两个扁指
	3. 舌位: 舌尖抵紧下牙齿

[ɔ] 后元音
后元音, 即舌后部 (舌根) 活动. [ɔ] 音与普通话中的 "凹" 音相似, 但不相同. 普通话中的 "凹" 音太放松, 而发后元音 [ɔ] 音时, 口是大圆形, 舌头平伸于口中, 舌前部和舌中部都不要碰到上齿和下齿, 舌后部要下压, 尽量要向外放音. [ɔ] 是短元音. 发音结束时, 仍然保持原来的口型, 不要闭嘴.

发音三要素	1. 唇势: 大圆形　　　2. 齿距: 两个半扁指
	3. 舌位: 舌头平伸于口中, 舌前部和舌中部都不要碰到上齿和下齿, 发音时舌后部下压.

[ʌ] 中元音
中元音, 即舌中部（舌端）活动. [ʌ] 音与普通话中的 "呵" 音相似, 但不相同. 普通话中的 "呵" 音太长, 开口太大, 而中元音 [ʌ] 音是短元音. 发音结束时, 仍然保持原来的口型, 不要闭嘴.

发音三要素	1. 唇势: 扁　　　　　2. 齿距: 两个扁指
	3. 舌位: 舌头平伸于口中, 舌前部不要碰到上齿和下齿, 舌中部在发音时抬高

[e] 前元音
前元音, 即舌前部 (舌尖) 活动. [e] 音与普通话中的 "艾" 音相似, 但不相同. 普通话中的 "艾" 音太长, 而前元音 [e] 音是短元音.发音结

束时, 舌尖仍然抵住下牙齿.		
发音三要素	1. 唇势: 扁	2. 齿距: 一个扁指
	3. 舌位: 舌尖抵紧下牙齿	

[i] 前元音		
前元音, 即舌前部 (舌尖) 活动. [i] 音是元音字母 A a 的尾音. 不要发成普通话中的 "一" 音, 因为 "一" 音太长, 而 [i] 音是短元音. [i] 音是 [ei] 音的尾音, 并不是 [i:] 音的短音. 发音结束时, 舌尖仍然抵住下牙齿.		
发音三要素	1. 唇势: 扁	2. 齿距: 半个扁指
	3. 舌位: 舌尖抵紧下牙齿	

English Pronunciation for Chinese Speakers

第七课　　练习
Lesson Seven　　Exercises

1.	什么叫闭音节	
2.	闭音节的读音规则是什么	

3.	闭音节的拼读练习						
	[æ]	[æ d]	[æ z]	[æ t]	[t æ p]	[p æ t]	[s æ d]
	[ɔ]	[ɔ f]	[ɔ k s]	[ɔ d]	[d ɔ g]	[g ɔ t]	[f ɔ g]
	[ʌ]	[ʌ p]	[ʌ s]	[ʌ t]	[p ʌ b]	[b ʌ t]	[d ʌ k]
	[e]	[e b]	[e g]	[e p]	[b e d]	[s e t]	[t e s t]
	[i]	[i t]	[i z]	[i f]	[pit]	[sit]	[did]

4.	朗读下列单词并写出音标								
	add		pot		but		set		did
	pit		best		pub		sock		tap
	bus		tip		desk		soft		dad
	bus		tip		desk		soft		dad

第八课 重读 R 音节

定义	一个元音字母 + 一个 r 的音节叫 r 音节（在单音节词中）
读音规则	ar 读 [ɑ:]　　　or 读 [ɔ:]　　　　　ur 读 [ə:] er 读 [ə:]　　　ir 读 [ə:]

元音字母+r 辅音字母	ar [ɑ:]	or [ɔ:]	ur [ə:]	er [ə:]	ir(yr) [ə:]
p [p]	park	pork	purp	perk	pirn
b [b]	bark	bord	burg	berg	bird
t [t]	tar	tort	turf	term	stir
d [d]	dart	dorp	durst	derv	dirt

读熟，读准三个长元音音素	
ar [ɑ:]	Bard parked Harp's car in Dart's car parking.
or [ɔ:]	This fork is for Port and that fork is for Port.
ur [ə:]	Urban met his nurse in Church on Thursday.
er [ə:]	Ferns and Herb serve Hertz earnestly.
ir [ə:]	The third girl will buy a purple fur skirt on her birthday first.

为什么叫 R 音节	因为单词中只有一个元音字母 + 一个 R 结尾的音节。

某些辅音字母的读音：

辅 音 字 母	读 音	例		词
H h	[h]	hard	help	hate
W w	[w]	we	why	wave
Y y	[j]	yes	yet	York
R r	[r]	red	read	risk

重读 R 音节的特殊情况

1. war 读 [wɔ:]　　　　2. wor 读 [wə:]

重读 R 音节的特殊情况	读 音	例		词
war	[wɔ:]	war	ward	warm
wor	[wə:]	word	work	world

元音音素: [ɑ:] [ɔ:] [ə:]

[ɑ:] 后元音
后元音, 即舌后部 (舌根) 活动. [ɑ:] 音与普通话中的"啊"音相似, 但不相同. 普通话中的"啊"音太放松, 而发后元音 [ɑ:] 音时, 口全开, 舌头平伸于口中. 舌前部和舌中部都不要碰到上齿和下齿, 舌后部要下压. [ɑ:] 是长元音, 发音结束时, 仍然保持原来的口型, 不要闭嘴.

发音三要素	1. 唇势: 口全开, 椭圆形 2. 齿距: 三个扁指 3. 舌位: 舌头平伸于口中, 舌前部和舌中部都不要碰到上齿和下齿, 发音时舌后部下压

[ɔ:] 后元音
后元音, 即舌后部 (舌根) 活动. [ɔ:] 音与普通话中的"奥"音相似, 但不相同. 普通话中的"奥"音太放松, 而发后元音 [ɔ:] 音时, 口是大圆形, 舌头平伸于口中, 舌前部和舌中部都不要碰到上齿和下齿, 舌后部要下压, 尽量要向外放音. [ɔ:] 是长元音. 发音结束时, 仍然保持原来的口型, 不要闭嘴.

发音三要素	1. 唇势: 大圆形 2. 齿距: 两个半扁指 3. 舌位: 舌头平伸于口中, 舌前部和舌中部都不要碰到上齿和下齿, 发音时舌后部下压

[ə:] 中元音
中元音, 即舌中部 (舌端) 活动. [ə:] 音与普通话中"饿"音相似, 但不相同. 普通话中的"饿"音太放松, 而发中元音 [ə:] 音时, 口腔稍紧张. [ə:] 是长元音, 发音结束时, 仍然保持原来的口型, 不要闭嘴.

发音三要素	1. 唇势: 扁 2. 齿距: 两个扁指 3. 舌位: 舌头平伸于口中, 舌前部不要碰到上齿和下齿, 舌中部在发音时抬高

English Pronunciation for Chinese Speakers

辅音音素: [h] [w] [r]

[h] 声门摩擦音	
发音时,用声门挡住气流,此时,憋住一口气,形成阻力,不能卷舌,要平伸于口中,不能碰到上齿和下齿,然后让气流从声门冲出,摩擦成音. [h] 音与普通话中的"喝"的声母音相似,但不相同. 要去掉"喝"的声母音的尾音,还要让气流从声门冲出,摩擦成 [h] 音. 发音结束时,可以松口气,但是要保持发音时的口型,不要闭嘴. 它是清辅音.	
发音三要素	1. 唇势: 扁　　　　　2. 齿距: 一个扁指 3. 舌位: 平伸于口中

[w] 舌后-软颚摩擦音	
发音时,舌后和软颚间要有空隙,此时,憋住一口气,形成阻力,不能卷舌,要平伸于口中,不能碰到上齿和下齿,然后让气流从舌后和软颚间冲出,摩擦成音. [w] 音与普通话中的"窝"的声母音相似,但不相同. 要去掉"窝"的声母音的尾音,还要让气流从舌后和软颚间冲出,摩擦成 [w] 音. 发音结束时,可以松口气,但是要保持发音时的口型,不要闭嘴. 它是浊辅音.	
发音三要素	1. 唇势: 圆　　　　　2. 齿距: 几乎闭合 3. 舌位: 平伸于口中

[r] 舌中 - 硬颚摩擦音	
发音时, 舌中和硬颚间要有空隙, 此时, 憋住一口气, 形成阻力, 不能卷舌, 要平伸于口中, 不要碰到上齿和下齿, 然后让气流从舌中和硬颚间冲出, 摩擦成音. [r] 音与普通话中的"若"的声母音相似, 但不相同. "若"是卷舌音, 是四声, 而国际音标 [r] 却不能卷舌, [r] 是一声. 发音结束时, 可以松口气, 但是要保持发音时的口型, 舌仍然平伸于口中, 不要闭嘴. 它是浊辅音.	
发音三要素	1. 唇势: 圆　　　　　2. 齿距: 几乎闭合 3. 舌位: 平伸于口中

第八课 Lesson Eight　　练习 Exercises

1.	什么叫 R 音节	
2.	R 音节的读音规则是什么	
3.	R 音节特殊情况是什么	

4. R 音节的拼读练习						
[ɑ :]	[ɑ : t]	[ɑ : s k]	[d ɑ : k]	[p ɑ: k]	[b ɑ:]	[h ɑ : d]
[ɔ :]	[f ɔ : d]	[s ɔ : t]	[k ɔ : k]	[p ɔ : k]	[f ɔ : k]	[h ɔ : s]
[ə :]	[b ə : g]	[p ə : s]	[f ə : st]	[k ə : b]	[s ə :]	[h ə : b]

5. R 音节特殊情况的拼读练习				
[w ɔ :]	[w ɔ :]	[w ɔ : d]	[w ɔ : p]	[w ɔ : t]
[w ə :]	[w ə : d]	[w ə : k]	[w ə : s]	[w ə : st]

6. 朗读下列单词并写出音标						
car		dirt		pork		curb	
fur		sort		verb		park	
war		dark		first		her	
word		bird		tort		perk	

7. 朗读下列单词并写出音标						
yoke		yet		yard		York	
rate		red		rude		rat	
ride		rod		fry		rock	

第九课 重读开音节，重读闭音节，重读R音节的总结

元音字母在重读开音节，重读闭音节，重读R音节中的读音					
重读音节＼元音字母	Aa	Oo	Uu	Ee	Ii(Yy)
重读开音节	[e i]	[ə u]	[j u:]	[i:]	[a i]
重读闭音节	[æ]	[ɔ]	[ʌ]	[e]	[i]
重读R音节	[ɑ:]	[ɔ:]	[ə:]	[ə:]	[ə:]

重读开音节，重读闭音节，重读R音节的比较 (1)				
辅音字母	元音字母	重读开音节	重读闭音节	重读R音节
s	a	[e i] save	[æ] sad	[ɑ:] SARS
	o	[ə u] sole	[ɔ] sock	[ɔ:] sort
	u	[j u:] supe	[ʌ] suck	[ə:] surf
	e	[i:] sene	[e] send	[ə:] serf
	i	[a i] site	[i] sit	[ə:] sir

重读开音节，重读闭音节，重读R音节的比较 (2)				
辅音字母	元音字母	重读开音节	重读闭音节	重读R音节
h	a	[e i] hate	[æ] hat	[ɑ:] hard
	o	[ə u] hope	[ɔ] hot	[ɔ:] horn
	u	[j u:] huge	[ʌ] hut	[ə:] hurt
	e	[i:] heme	[e] hen	[ə:] herb
	i	[a i] hide	[i] hid	[ə:] hirsute

第九课　　　　练习
Lesson Nine　　Exercises

1. 开音节，闭音节和 R 音节的综合拼读练习					
[e i]	[e i p]	[æ t]	[ɑ : t]	[w ɔ : t]	
[ə u]	[ə u k]	[ɔ f]	[p ɔ : t]	[w ə : d]	
[j u :]	[j u : s]	[ʌ s]	[f ə :]	[k ə : b]	
[i :]	[i : v]	[e g]	[p ə :]	[b ə : g]	
[a i]	[a i]	[s i t]	[f ə :s t]	[b ə : d]	

2. 朗读下列单词并写出音标							
ate		gap		part		ward	
ode		fox		cord		word	
use		dust		burst		hurt	
eve		nest		serf		verb	
side		disk		bird		first	

第十课 重读 Re 音节

定义：一个元音字母 + re 的音节叫 Re 音节 (在单音节词中)

读音规则：are [εə]　ore [ɔ:]　ure [juə]　ere [iə]　ire [aiə]

重读 Re 音节	读 音	例			词		
are	[εə]	care	fare	dare	ware	rare	hare
ore	[ɔ:]	core	bore	more	store	before	score
ure	[juə]	cure	pure	secure			
ere	[iə]	here	mere	sphere	adhere	severe	
ire	[aiə]	fire	hire	tire	fire	wire	require

元音音素 [ə] [u] [iə] [ɛə] [uə]

[ə] 中元音	
中元音,即舌中部(舌端)活动.[ə]音与普通话中的"阿"音相似,但不相同.普通话中的"阿"音太长,开口太大,而中元音[ə]音是短元音.发音结束时,仍然保持原来的口型,不要闭嘴.	
发音三要素	1. 唇势:扁　　　　　2. 齿距:两个扁指 3. 舌位:舌头平伸于口中,舌前部不要碰到上齿和下齿,舌中部在发音时抬高.

[u] 后元音	
后元音,即舌后部(舌根)活动.[u]音与普通话中的"屋"音相似,但不相同.普通话中的"屋"音太放松,而发后元音[u]音时,口是小圆形,舌头平伸于口中,舌前部和舌中部不要碰到上齿和下齿.发音时,舌后部要上抬,尽量向里拢音.[u]是短元音,发音结束时,仍然保持原来的口型,不要闭嘴.	
发音三要素	1. 唇势:小圆形　　　2. 齿距:一个半扁指 3. 舌位:舌头平伸于口中,舌前部和舌中部都不要碰到上齿和下齿,发音时舌后部上抬.

[iə] 开口双元音	
开口双元音[iə]是由第一个元音[i]向第二个元音[ə]滑动发音时,嘴型一定要从小到大滑动.[i]音是元音字母Aa的尾音;[ə]音与普通话中的"阿"音相似,但不相同.从[i]音向[ə]音滑动发音时,嘴型一定要从小到大滑动.发音结束时,齿距仍然是两个扁指,不要闭嘴.	
发音三要素	1. 唇势:扁　　2. 齿距:从半个扁指滑动到两个扁指 3. 舌位:发音时,从舌前部滑动到舌中部,以唇势:扁,齿距:两个扁指,舌位:舌中活动结束发[iə]音.

[ɛə] 开口双元音	
开口双元音 [ɛə] 是由第一个元音 [ɛ] 向第二个元音 [ə] 滑动发音时，嘴型一定要从小到大滑动. [ɛ] 音的齿距是一个半扁指，是介于元音 [æ] (两个扁指) 和 [e] (一个扁指) 之间的音. [ə] 音与普通话中的"阿"音相似，但不相同. 从 [ɛ] 音向 [ə] 音滑动发音时，嘴型一定要从小到大滑动. 发音结束时，齿距仍然是两个扁指，不要闭嘴.	
发音三要素	1. 唇势：扁　　2. 齿距：从一个半扁指滑动到两个扁指 3. 舌位：发音时，从舌前部滑动到舌中部，以唇势：扁，齿距：两个扁指，舌位：舌中活动结束发 [ɛə] 音.

[uə] 开口双元音	
开口双元音 [uə] 是由第一个元音 [u] 向第二个元音 [ə] 滑动发音时，嘴一定要从小到大滑动. [u] 音与普通话中的"屋"音相似，但不相同，[ə] 音与普通话中的"阿"音相似，也不相同. 从 [u] 音向 [ə] 音滑动发音时，嘴型一定要从小到大滑动. 发音结束时,齿距仍然是两个扁指,不要闭嘴.	
发音三要素	1. 唇势：从小圆到扁 2. 齿距：从一个半扁指滑动到两个扁指 3. 舌位：发音时，从舌后部滑动到舌中部，以唇势：扁，齿距：两个扁指，舌位：舌中活动结束发 [uə] 音.

第十课　　　　练习
Lesson Ten　　　Exercises

1.	什么叫 Re 音节	
2.	Re 音节的读音规则是什么	

3. Re 音节的拼读练习				
[ɛ ə]	[k ɛ ə]	[f ɛ ə]	[d ɛ ə]	[h ɛ ə]
[ɔ:]	[b ɔ:]	[k ɔ:]	[f ɔ:]	[s t ɔ:]
[j u ə]	[k j u ə]	[p j u ə]	[s i k j u ə]	
[i ə]	[h i ə]	[s f i ə]	[s i v i ə]	
[a i ə]	[f a i ə]	[h a i ə]	[t a i ə]	[w a i ə]

4. 朗读下列单词并写出音标							
pare		score		pure		here	
wire		dare		bore		hire	

5. 辅音音素和元音音素的拼读练习					
[ə]	ago	about	aware	comma	central
[u]	book	look	took	put	push
[i ə]	ear	beer	dear	hear	here
[ɛ ə]	bare	tare	pare	fair	pair
[u ə]	poor	boor	tour	dour	sure

第十一课

部分辅音和部分辅音字母以及部分辅音字母组合在单词中的读音

部分辅音字母在单词中的读音：

辅音字母	读 音	例 词		
L l	[l]	bill	pill	dull
		silk	molk	tilt
		file	tile	pile
L l 在词首或在元音前	[l]	lake	lost	luck
		close	glad	slope
M m	[m]	sum	gum	bum
		pump	sump	tump
		lime	same	time
M m 在词首或在元音前	[m]	make	mop	must
		small	smart	smell
N n	[n]	loan	pain	gain
		cane	sane	bane
		lind	since	enter
N n 在词首或在元音前	[n]	name	not	nut
		sneak	snack	snow

部分辅音字母组合在单词中的读音：

辅音字母组合	读 音	例 词		
ng	[ŋ]	sang	song	lung
nk	[ŋk]	bank	sink	rank

辅音音素 [l] [m] [n] [ŋ]

[l] 舌前 - 齿龈舌侧音或旁流音	
辅音字母 l 在单词中发 [l] 音. 发音时, 舌尖抵紧上齿龈, 憋住一口气, 形成阻力, 然后让气流从口腔中的舌尖和齿龈两旁突然冲出, 摩擦成 [l] 音. 发音时, 口腔部位与发 [t], [d] 和 [n] 音的口腔部位相同. [l] 音与普通话中"欧"音相似, 但不相同. 发音结束时, 可以松口气, 但是要保持发音时的口型, 舌尖离开上齿龈, 不要闭嘴. 它是浊辅音.	
发音三要素	1. 唇势: 扁　　　　2. 齿距: 几乎闭合 3. 舌位: 舌尖抵紧上齿龈

l [l]	
辅音字母 l 在词首或元音前发 [l] 音. 发音时, 舌尖抵紧上齿龈, 憋住一口气, 形成阻力, 然后让气流从口腔中的舌尖和齿龈两旁突然冲出, 摩擦成音. 音从舌两旁流出音时, 舌尖离开上齿龈. 发音时, 口腔部位与发 [t], [d] 和 [n] 音的口腔部位相同. [l] 音与普通话中的 "了" 的声母音相似, 但不相同. 要去掉"了"的声母音的尾音, 还要让气流从口腔中的舌尖和齿龈两旁突然冲出, 摩擦成 [l] 音去拼后面的元音. 发音结束时, 可以松口气, 但是要保持发音时的口型, 舌尖离开上齿龈, 不要闭嘴. 它是浊辅音.	
发音三要素	1. 唇势: 扁　　　　2. 齿距: 几乎闭合 3. 舌位: 舌尖抵紧上齿龈, 音从舌两旁流出音后, 舌尖离开上齿龈

m [m]

辅音字母 m 在词首或元音前发 [m] 音发音时, 双唇紧闭, 憋住一口气, 不能卷舌, 要平伸于口中, 不能碰到上齿和下齿, 也不能让气流从口腔中出来. 要让气流从鼻腔发出 [m] 音. 发音时, 口腔部位与发 [p] 和 [b] 音的口腔部位相同. [m] 在拼它后边的元音时,它的音与普通话拼音中的"m"音相似, 但要去掉 "m" 音的尾音, 还要双唇紧闭, 憋住一口气, 让气流从鼻腔发出 [m] 音来拼它后面的元音. 它是浊辅音.

发音三要素	1. 唇势: 双唇紧闭　　2. 齿距: 几乎闭合 3. 舌位: 平伸于口中

[m] 双唇-鼻音

辅音字母 m 在单词中发 [m] 音. 发音时, 双唇紧闭, 憋住一口气, 不能卷舌, 要平伸于口中, 不能碰到上齿和下齿, 也不能让气流从口腔中出来, 要让气流从鼻腔发出 [m] 音. 发音时, 口腔部位与发 [p] 和 [b] 音的口腔部位相同. [m] 音与普通话中的 "牡" 的声母音的一声音相似, 而 "牡" 音在普通话中是三声音, 但与 "牡" 的声母音不相同. 要去掉 "牡" 的声母音的尾音, 还要双唇紧闭, 憋住一口气, 让气流从鼻腔发出 [m] 音. 发音结束时, 可以松口气, 但是要保持发音时的口型, 不要张开口. 它是浊辅音.

发音三要素	1. 唇势: 双唇紧闭　　2. 齿距: 几乎闭合 3. 舌位: 平伸于口中

[n] 舌前-齿龈鼻音

辅音字母 n 在单词中发 [n] 音. 发音时, 舌尖抵紧上齿龈, 憋住一口气, 形成阻力, 不能让气流从口腔中出来, 要让气流从鼻腔中发出 [n] 音. 发音时, 口腔部位与发 [t], [d] 和 [l] 音的口腔部位相同. [n] 音与普通话中的 "呢" 的声母音相似, 但不相同, 要去掉 "呢" 的声母音的尾音, 还要舌尖抵紧上齿龈, 憋住一口气, 形成阻力, 让气流从鼻腔中发出 [n] 音. 发音结束时, 可以松口气,但是要保持发音时的口型, 不要闭嘴. 舌尖不要离开上齿龈. 它是浊辅音.

发音三要素	1. 唇势: 扁　　2. 齿距: 几乎闭合 3. 舌位: 舌尖抵紧上齿龈

n [n]
辅音字母 n 在词首或元音前发 [n] 音. 发音时, 舌尖抵紧上齿龈, 憋住一口气, 形成阻力, 不能让气流从口腔中出来, 要让气流从鼻腔中发出 [n] 音. 发音时, 口腔部位与发 [t], [d] 和 [l] 音的口腔部位相同. [n] 在拼它后边的元音时, 它的音与普通话拼音中的"n"音相似, 但要去掉 "n" 音的尾音, 还要舌尖抵紧上齿龈, 憋住一口气, 形成阻力, 让气流从鼻腔中发出 [n] 音来拼它后边的元音. 它是浊辅音.
	1. 唇势: 扁　　　　　　　2. 齿距: 几乎闭合 3. 舌位: 舌尖抵紧上齿龈

[ŋ] 舌后-软腭鼻音	
发音时, 舌跟贴近软腭, 憋住一口气, 形成阻力, 不能让气流从口腔中出来, 要让气流从鼻腔中发出 [ŋ] 音. 发音时, 口腔部位与发 [k] 和 [g] 音的口腔部位相同. [ŋ] 音与普通话拼音中的 "ing" 音的尾音相似, 但不相同. 得让你的舌跟贴近软腭, 憋住一口气, 形成阻力, 让气流从鼻腔中发出 [ŋ] 音. 发音结束时, 可以松口气, 但是要保持发音时的口型, 不要闭嘴. 舌跟和软腭间仍然有空隙. 它是浊辅音.	
发音三要素	1. 唇势: 扁　　　　　　　2. 齿距: 半个扁指 3. 舌位: 舌跟贴近软腭

第十一课　　　　　　练习
Lesson Eleven　　　　Exercises

	辅音音素和元音音素的拼读练习		
[l]	late	lap	lark
	blade	glad	fly
[l]	milk	silk	tilt
	bill	pill	till
	file	tile	pile
[m]	make	mad	mark
	smoke	smart	smile
[m]	same	lime	time
	bum	plum	slim
	pump	lump	bump
[n]	name	nap	nor
	snake	sneak	snap
[n]	line	fine	pine
	bin	pin	tin
	Linda	since	pinch
[ŋ]	sing	lung	wing
	bank	sink	rank

第十二课

辅音字母 Jj 在单词中的读音								
辅 音 字 母	读 音	例 词						
J j	[dʒ]	jade	joke	jeep	jack	jet	job	just

部分辅音字母组合在单词中的读音					
辅音字母组合	读 音	例 词			
th 在实词中	[θ]	theme	thick	theft	thank
		path	north	south	oath
th 在功能词中	[ð]	this	that	these	those
		with	lathe		
sh	[ʃ]	sheet	ship	ash	cash
	[ʒ]	beige	garage	Jean	
ch	[tʃ]	cheap	chess	beach	reach
tr	[tr]	treat	trip	trust	try
dr	[dr]	dream	drill	dress	dry
ts	[ts]	pets	cats	hats	sits
tes	[ts]	plates	grates	hates	gates
ds	[dz]	beds	kids	hands	lids
des	[dz]	spades	grades	blades	

部分元音字母组合和元,辅音字母组合在单词中的读音						
字 母 组 合	读 音	例 词				
ou	[au]	loud	proud	cloud	mouth	blouse
ow	[au]	how	now	cow	plow	cowl
oi	[ɔi]	soil	boil	foil	coil	void
oy	[ɔi]	boy	soy	toy	joy	employ
our	[uə]	tour	gourmet	gourd	dour	bourse

辅音音素[θ][ð][ʃ][ʒ][ts][dz][tr][dr][tʃ][dʒ]

[θ] 舌前 - 上齿外摩擦音		
[θ]和[ð]是一对清,浊辅音.[θ]发音时,舌前抵紧上齿外,憋住一口气,形成阻力,然后让气流从舌前和上齿间冲出,摩擦成音.发音时,口腔部位与发[ð]音的口腔部位相同.普通话中没有[θ]音,可以用舌前抵紧上齿外,憋住一口气,形成阻力,然后用力让气流从舌前和上齿间摩擦成一个相似于普通话拼音中的"s"音.与普通话拼音中的"s"音不相同之处在于,要让舌前抵紧上齿外,让气流从舌前和上齿间摩擦发出[θ]音.发音结束时,舌前仍然抵上齿外,舌前不要离开上齿外.它是清辅音.		
发音三要素	1. 唇势: 扁　　　　　2. 齿距: 舌的厚度 3. 舌位: 舌前抵紧上齿外		

[ð] 舌前 - 上齿外摩擦音		
[θ]和[ð]是一对清,浊辅音.[ð]发音时,舌前抵紧上齿外,憋住一口气,形成阻力,然后让气流从舌前和上齿间冲出,摩擦成音.发音时,口腔部位与发[θ]音的口腔部位相同.普通话中没有[ð]音,你可以用舌前抵紧上齿外,憋住一口气,形成阻力,然后用力让气流从舌前和上齿间摩擦成一个相似于普通话拼音中的"r"音,但与普通话拼音中的"r"音不相同.普通话拼音中的"r"音是卷舌音,而国际音标[ð]却不能卷舌.发音时,要让舌前抵紧上齿外,让气流从舌前和上齿间摩擦才能发出[ð]音.发音结束时,舌前仍然抵上齿外,舌前不要离开上齿外.它是浊辅音.		
发音三要素	1. 唇势: 扁　　　　　2. 齿距: 舌的厚度 3. 舌位: 舌前抵紧上齿外		

[ʃ] 舌中 - 硬颚摩擦音		
[ʃ]和[ʒ]是一对清,浊辅音.[ʃ]发音时,舌中和硬颚靠近,但要有间隙.此时,憋住一口气,形成阻力,舌不能卷,要平伸于口中,不能碰到上齿和下齿,然后让气流从舌中和硬颚间冲出,摩擦成音.在发音时,口腔部位与下面的[ʒ]的发音口腔部位相同.由于普通话中没有[ʃ]音,需要让舌中和硬颚靠近,但要有间隙.此时,憋住一口气,形成阻力,然		

后用力让气流从舌中和硬颚间摩擦成一个相似于普通话拼音中的"sh"音. 但与普通话拼音中"sh"音不相同. 普通话拼音中"sh"音是卷舌音. 而 [ʃ] 却不能卷舌.要领是让舌中和硬颚靠近,但要有间隙,让气流从舌中和硬颚间摩擦才能发出 [ʃ] 音. 发音结束时,舌中和硬颚间仍然有空隙, 保持发音时口型, 不要闭嘴.它是清辅音.

发音三要素	1. 唇势: 圆　　　　　　　2. 齿距: 几乎闭合 3. 舌位: 平伸于口中

[ʒ] 舌中 - 硬颚摩擦音
[ʃ] 和 [ʒ] 是一对清, 浊辅音. [ʒ] 发音时, 舌中和硬颚靠近, 但有间隙, 此时, 憋住一口气, 形成阻力, 舌不能卷, 要平伸于口中, 不能碰到上齿和下齿, 然后让气流从舌中和硬颚间冲出, 摩擦成音. 在发音时, 口腔部位与发 [ʃ] 音口腔部位相同. 由于普通话中没有 [ʒ] 音, 需要让舌中和硬颚靠近, 但要有间隙.此时, 憋住一口气, 形成阻力, 然后用力让气流从舌中和硬颚间摩擦成一个相似于普通话拼音中的"r"音.但与普通话拼音中的"r"音不相同.普通话拼音中的"r"音是卷舌音, 而国际音标 [ʒ] 却不能卷舌.要领是让舌中和硬颚靠近, 但要有间隙, 让气流从舌中和硬颚间摩擦才能发出 [ʒ] 音.发音结束时, 舌中和硬颚间仍然有空隙, 保持发音时的口型, 不要闭嘴. 它是浊辅音.

发音三要素	1. 唇势: 圆　　　　　　　2. 齿距: 几乎闭合 3. 舌位: 平伸于口中

[tr] 破擦音 (既有爆破音又有摩擦音)
[tr] 和 [dr] 是一对清, 浊辅音.发 [tr] 音时, 舌尖抵紧上齿龈, 憋住一口气, 形成阻力, 然后发 [t] 音, 但不要发出 [t] 音, 就发 [r] 音, 使之摩擦成 [tr] 音.发音时, 口腔部位与发 [dr] 音的口腔部位相同. [tr] 音与普通话中的"戳"音相似, 但不相同.普通话中的"戳"是卷舌音, 而 [tr] 却不能有卷舌音.要领是破擦音 [tr] 中的 [t] 音要不完全爆破, 而 [r] 音却要摩擦.发音结束时, 可以松口气, 但是舌仍然平伸于口中, 不要闭嘴.它是清辅音.

发音三要素	1. 唇势: 圆　　　　　　2. 齿距: 几乎闭合
	3. 舌位: 首先舌尖抵紧上齿龈, 然后舌中和硬颚间要有空隙.

[dr] 破擦音 (既有爆破音又有摩擦音)
[tr] 和 [dr] 是一对清,浊辅音. [dr] 发音时, 舌尖抵紧上齿龈, 憋住一口气, 形成阻力, 然后发 [d] 音, 但不要发出 [d] 音, 就发 [r] 音, 使之摩擦成 [dr] 音.发音时, 口腔部位与发 [tr] 音的口腔部位相同. [dr] 音与普通话中的 "桌" 音相似, 但不相同. 普通话中的 "桌" 是卷舌音, 而 [dr] 却不能有卷舌音. 要领是破擦音 [dr] 中的 [d] 音要不完全爆破, 而 [r] 音却要摩擦. 发音结束时, 可以松口气, 但是舌仍然平伸于口中, 不要闭嘴. 它是浊辅音.

发音三要素	1. 唇势: 圆　　　　　　2. 齿距: 几乎闭合
	3. 舌位: 首先舌尖抵紧上齿龈, 然后舌中和硬颚间要有空隙

[ts] 破擦音 (既有爆破音又有摩擦音)
[ts] 和 [dz] 是一对清,浊辅音. [ts] 发音时, 舌尖抵紧上齿龈, 憋住一口气, 形成阻力, 然后让你的舌头顺着上齿龈一直刮止下牙齿摩擦成 [ts] 音. 发音时, 口腔部位与发 [dz] 音的口腔部位相同. [ts] 音与普通话拼音中的 "c" 音相似, 但不相同.要领是破擦音 [ts] 中的 [t]音要不完全爆破, 而 [s] 音却要摩擦. 发音结束时, 舌尖仍然抵下齿, 舌尖不要离开下齿.它是清辅音.

发音三要素	1. 唇势: 扁　　　　　　2. 齿距: 几乎闭合
	3. 舌位: 舌尖抵紧上齿龈, 然后舌头顺着上齿龈一直止下牙齿摩擦成音

[dz] 破擦音 (既有爆破音又有摩擦音)
[ts] 和 [dz] 是一对清, 浊辅音. [dz] 发音时, 舌尖抵紧上齿龈, 憋住一口气, 形成阻力, 然后用舌头顺着上齿龈一直刮止下牙齿摩擦成 [dz]

音.发音时,口腔部位与发 [ts] 音的口腔部位相同. [dz] 音与普通话拼音中的 "z" 音相似,但不相同.要领是破擦音 [dz] 中的 [d] 音要不完全爆破,而 [z] 音却要摩擦.发音结束时,舌尖仍然抵下齿,舌尖不要离开下齿.它是浊辅音.

发音三要素	1. 唇势: 扁　　　　　　　　2. 齿距: 几乎闭合 3. 舌位: 舌尖抵紧上齿龈,然后舌头顺着上齿龈一直刮止下牙齿摩擦成音.

[tʃ] 破擦音 (既有爆破音又有摩擦音)

[tʃ] 和 [dʒ] 是一对清,浊辅音. [tʃ] 发音时,舌尖抵紧上齿龈,憋住一口气,形成阻力,然后发 [t] 音,但不要发出 [t] 音,就发 [ʃ] 音,使之摩擦成 [tʃ] 音.发音时,口腔部位与发[dʒ]音的口腔部位相同. [tʃ] 音与普通话拼音中的 "ch" 音相似,但不相同.普通话拼音中的 "ch" 是卷舌音,而 [tʃ] 却不能有卷舌音.要领是破擦音 [tʃ] 中的 [t] 音要不完全爆破,而 [ʃ] 音却要摩擦.发音结束时,可以松口气,但是舌仍然要平伸于口中,不要闭嘴.它是清辅音.

发音三要素	1. 唇势: 圆　　　　　　　　2. 齿距: 几乎闭合 3. 舌位: 首先舌尖抵紧上齿龈,然后舌中和硬颚间要有空隙

[dʒ] 破擦音 (既有爆破音又有摩擦音)

[tʃ] 和 [dʒ] 是一对清,浊辅音. [dʒ] 发音时,舌尖抵紧上齿龈,憋住一口气,形成阻力,然后发 [d] 音,但不要发出 [d] 音,就发 [ʒ] 音,使之摩擦成 [dʒ] 音.发音时,口腔部位与发 [tʃ] 音的口腔部位相同. [dʒ] 音与普通话拼音中的 "zh" 音相似,但不相同.普通话拼音中的 "zh" 是卷舌音,而 [dʒ] 却不能有卷舌音.要领是破擦音 [dʒ]中的 [d] 音要不完全爆破,而 [ʒ] 音却要摩擦.发音结束时,可以松口气,但是舌仍然要平伸于口中,不要闭嘴.它是浊辅音.

发音三要素	1. 唇势: 圆　　　2. 齿距: 几乎闭合
	3. 舌位: 首先舌尖抵紧上齿龈, 然后舌中和硬颚间要有空隙

元音音素 [au] [ɔi]

[au] 合口双元音
合口双元音 [au] 是由第一个元音 [a] 向第二个元音 [u] 滑动发音时, 嘴型一定要从大到小滑动. [au] 音与普通话拼音中的 "啊" 和后元音 [u] 音相似, 但不相同. 普通话拼音中的 "啊" 音太放松, 而合口双元音中的 [a] 音时, 口全开, 舌下压. 发音结束时, 嘴型是小圆.

发音三要素	1. 唇势: 嘴型从口全开滑动到小圆
	2. 齿距: 从三个扁指滑动到一个半个扁指
	3. 舌位: 发音时, 舌后部从下压放音滑动到舌后部上抬拢音. 以唇势: 小圆, 齿距: 一个半扁指, 舌位: 舌后部上抬拢音结束发音.

[ɔi] 合口双元音
合口双元音 [ɔi] 是由第一个元音 [ɔ] 向第二个元音 [i] 滑动发音时, 嘴型一定要从大到小滑动. [ɔi] 音与普通话拼音中的 "凹" 和前元音 [i] 音相似, 但不相同. 普通话拼音中的 "凹" 音太放松, 而发合口双元音中的 [ɔ] 音时, 口型大圆放音, 后舌活动. 发音结束时, 舌尖仍然抵下牙齿, 不要闭嘴.

发音三要素	1. 唇势: 嘴型从大圆到很扁
	2. 齿距: 从两个半扁指滑动到半个扁指
	3. 舌位: 发音时, 从舌后部滑动到舌前部, 以唇势: 扁, 齿距: 半个扁指, 舌位: 舌尖紧抵下齿结束发音

第十二课　　练习
Lesson Twelve　　Exercises

\multicolumn{7}{c}{辅音音素和元音音素的拼读练习}						
[θ]	theme	thick	theft	thank	thud	third
[ð]	these	this	them	that	thus	there
[ʃ]	sheet	ship	shelf	sham	shut	share
[ʒ]	beige	garage	measure	pleasure	treasure	vision
[ts]	sits	pits	pets	tests	grates	plates
[dz]	dream	drill	dress	drag	drug	draft
[tr]	treat	trip	trend	tract	trust	trade
[dr]	dream	drill	dress	drag	drug	draft
[tʃ]	cheap	chips	chess	shat	church	chair
[dʒ]	jeep	jet	jack	just	jade	joy

第十三课

重读音节字母组合	是英语的五大读音规则之一
重读音节字母组合分三类	1. 重读音节元音字母组合 2. 重读音节辅音字母组合 3. 重读音节元-辅音字母组合
重读音节元字母组合	由两个元音字母组合在一起，在单词中发一个或几个固定的音素. 例如: ea 和 au.

元音字母组合 e a 在单词中通常有四种读音			
元音字母组合 ea	读音	例 词	
多数情况	[i :]	sea	tea	eat
少数情况	[e]	head	bread	weather
特殊情况	[ei]	great	break	steak
极特殊情况	[iə]	real	really	realty

(其它元音字母组合见附表)	
重读音节辅音字母组合	由两个或两个以上的辅音字母组合在一起，在单词中发一个或几个固定的音素. 例如: ch, sh 和 tch

辅音字母组合 ch 在单词中有三种读音			
辅音字母组合 ch	读 音	例 词		
多数情况	[tʃ]	chair	lunch	bench
少数情况	[ʃ]	chef	chalet	machine
特殊情况	[k]	Christmas	chemist	school

	(其它辅音字母组合见附表)			
重读音节元-辅音字母组合	由元音字母和辅音字母组合在一起,在单词中发一个或几个固定的音素。例如: ew, igh 和 tory.			
元-辅音字母组合 igh 在单词中读 [a i] 音				
元,辅音字母组合	读 音	例 词		
igh	[ai]	might	sight	light	right
(其它元-辅音字母组合见附表)				

十三课
Lesson Thirteen

练习
Exercises

1.	重读音节读音规则有几种?	
2.	重读音节字母组合有几种?	
3.	写出5个开音节的单词:	
4.	写出5个闭音节的单词:	
5.	写出5个R音节的单词:	
6.	写出5个Re音节的单词:	
7.	写出5个元音字母组合的单词:	
8.	写出5个辅音字母组合的单词:	
9.	写出5个元,辅音字母组合的单词:	

第十四课

辅音字母在单词中的三种读音	1. 一个字母在单词中只有一种读音的辅音字母
	2. 一个字母在单词中有两种读音的辅音字母
	3. 一个字母在单词中发两个音的辅音字母

一个字母在单词中有两种读音的辅音字母					
辅音字母		读音	例		词
C c	在 e, i, y 前	[s]	cent	cite	cycle
	在 a, o, u 前	[k]	cake	code	cute
	或其它场合		clock	clinic	bicycle
G g	在 e, i, y 前	[dʒ]	germ	gibe	gym
	在 a, o, u 前	[g]	gate	go	gum
	或其它场合		glad	gray	pig
L l	在单词中	[l]	bill	pill	dull
			file	tile	pile
			silk	milk	tilt
L l	在词首	[l]	late	lot	lark
	在元音前		close	globe	fly
M m	在单词中	[m]	sum	slim	home
			lime	time	same
			pump	sump	tump
M m	在词首或在元音前	[m]	make	mop	mark
			small	smart	smoke
N n	在单词中	[n]	line	fine	pine
			loan	gain	pain
			enter	since	Linda
N n	在词首	[n]	name	not	nine
	在元音前		snake	snack	snap
S s	在词首	[s]	stay	sit	sky

	在元音后	[z]	has	is	was

一个字母在单词中发两个音的辅音字母				
辅 音 字 母	读 音	例		词
X x	[ks]	box	fox	fix
X x 在元音前	[gz]	example	exact	exam

Linan Shi & Shasha Shi

第十四课　　练习
Lesson Fourteen　　Exercises

1.	抄写一个字母在单词中只有一种读音的辅音字母 (抄写一遍)
2.	抄写一个字母在单词中发两个音的辅音字母 (抄写三遍)
3.	抄写一个字母在单词中有两种读音的辅音字母 (抄写两遍)

第十五课

辅音字母组合	读 音	例 词		
ch	[tʃ]	cheap	bench	lunch
	[ʃ]	chef	machine	chalet
	[k]	Christmas	school	chemical
ck	[k]	back	sick	pack
gh	[f]	cough	enough	laugh
	[g]	ghost	ghetto	ghee
gn	[n]	foreign	design	campaign
kn	[n]	knife	knock	know
ng	[ŋ]	long	song	sing
nk	[ŋk]	bank	sink	thank
ph	[f]	phone	phase	graph
sh	[ʃ]	shop	wish	fish
tch	[tʃ]	watch	match	patch
tw	[tw]	twice	twist	twin
wh	[w]	what	when	where
	[h]	who	whole	whose
wr	[r]	wrong	write	wrist
th	[θ]	third	think	cloth
	[ð]	this	that	with
tr	[tr]	try	treat	trip
dr	[dr]	dry	dream	drill
ts	[ts]	cats	hats	pats
tes	[ts]	plates	grates	hates
ds	[dz]	beds	hands	stands
des	[dz]	grades	spades	blades

重读辅音字母连缀的读音规则:	两个或两个以上的辅音字母连缀组合在一起, 发固定的音.		
辅音字母连缀	读 音	例	词
sc	[sk]	scream	screw	scar
sk	[sk]	sky	skin	skirt
sl	[sl]	slope	slow	slim
sm	[sm]	smoke	smart	smell
sn	[sn]	sneak	snap	sneeze
sp	[sp]	spring	spy	speak
sq	[sk]	square	squeeze	squirrel
st	[st]	steel	star	state
str	[str]	street	strong	strike
sw	[sw]	swim	sweep	sweet
bl	[bl]	bloom	block	black
br	[br]	bring	bright	break
cl	[kl]	clear	clean	clear
cr	[kr]	cry	cream	cross
fl	[fl]	floor	fleet	fly
fr	[fr]	free	fry	fresh
gl	[gl]	glue	glad	globe
gr	[gr]	green	gray	ground
pl	[pl]	play	plus	plan
pr	[pr]	pray	price	proud

English Pronunciation for Chinese Speakers

第十五课　　　练习
Lesson Fifteen　　Exercises

1.	抄写重读音节辅音字母组合在单词中的常用的读音规则表: (抄写一遍)
2.	听写重读音节辅音字母组合在单词中的常用的读音规则:

第十六课

重读音节元音字母组合在单词中的常用的读音规则			
元音字母组合	读 音	例 词		
ai	[ei]	aim	pain	rain
ai	[e]	said		
au	[ɔ:]	August	Autumn	author
ay	[ei]	bay	say	pay
ay	[e]	says		
oa	[əu]	oak	load	road
oe		doe	foe	toe
oi	[ɔi]	oil	boil	soil
oo	[u:]	fool	too	noon
oo	[u]	book	look	took
oo	[ʌ]	blood	flood	
ou	[au]	loud	out	mouth
ou	[u:]	group	you	soup
ou	[ʌ]	young	country	touch
ou	[ɔ]	cough		
oy	[ɔi]	boy	toy	soy
uy	[ai]	buy	guy	
ea	[i:]	sea	tea	pea
ea	[e]	head	bread	thread
ea	[ei]	great	steak	break
ea	[iə]	real	theatre	realtor
ee	[i:]	see	week	bee
ei		receive	receipt	ceiling
ei	[ei]	eight	veil	vein
ey		they	grey	hey
ey	[i:]	key		

ie	[ai]	pie	tie	lie
ie	[iː]	piece	field	sieve
ie	[aiə]	diet	piety	
ye	[ai]	dye	bye	lye

重读音节元,辅音字母组合在单词中的常用的读音规则			
元,辅音字母组合	读 音	例	词	
aft	[ɑːft]	after	afternoon	aftermath
air	[ɛə]	chair	hair	fair
aigh	[ei]	straight		
al	[ɔːl]	also	almost	already
al	[ɔː]	talk	chalk	walk
al	[ɑː]	half	calf	palm
all	[ɔːl]	mall	tall	ball
an	[æn]	fan	can	pan
ant	[ɑːnt]	plant	answer	slant
ance	[ɑːns]	dance	glance	dance
ask	[ɑːsk]	ask	flask	mask
asp	[ɑːsp]	rasp	grasp	gasp
ass	[ɑːs]	pass	class	glass
ast	[ɑːst]	past	last	fast
augh	[ɔː]	taught	caught	naught
aw	[ɔː]	law	paw	raw
oar		board	boar	soar
ol	[əu]	folk	yolk	folksy
ol	[əul]	bolt	bold	volt
old	[əuld]	sold	gold	fold
oll	[əu]	roll	stroll	toll
on	[ɔn]	fond	pond	bond
oor	[ɔː]	floor	door	

oor	[uə]	poor	boor	moor
ost	[əust]	post	host	most
oul	[u:]	could	would	should
oun	[aun]	round	found	pound
our	[auə]	hour	ours	ourself
our	[ɔ:]	your	court	four
our	[ə:]	journey		
our	[uə]	tour	gourd	dour
ough	[ɔ:]	thought	bought	fought
ow	[au]	how	now	power
ow	[əu]	grow	slow	bow
un	[ʌn]	fun	bun	sun
un	[ʌŋ]	hungry	uncle	punctual
ear	[iə]	hear	dear	fear
ear	[ɛə]	bear	pear	wear
ear	[ə:]	learn	earn	earth
eer	[iə]	deer	beer	leer
eigh	[ei]	weigh	weight	neighbor
eigh	[ai]	height		
en	[en]	end	ten	hen
ere	[iə]	mere	here	sere
ere	[ɛə]	there	where	therefore
ew	[u:]	flew	brew	lewd
ew	[ju:]	pew	mew	dew
ew	[əu]	sew	lewd	
igh	[ai]	light	night	sight
ild	[aild]	child	mild	wild
in	[in]	inch	pin	bin
dge	[dʒ]	badge	bridge	fridge
gu	[g]	guest	guitar	guard

English Pronunciation for Chinese Speakers

gu	[gw]	languish	anguish	linguist
qu	[kw]	quit	quarter	quite
que	[k]	unique	brusque	antique
the	[ð]	teethe	lathe	bathe
wa	[wɔ]	wash	watch	want

第十六课   练习
Lesson Sixteen   Exercises

1.	抄写重读音节元音字母组合在单词中的常用的读音规则表: (抄写一遍)
2.	听写重读音节元音字母组合在单词中的常用的读音规则:
3.	抄写重读音节元, 辅音字母组合在单词中的常用的读音规则表: (抄写一遍)
4.	听写重读音节元, 辅音字母组合在单词中的常用的读音规则

第十七课

音节的划分	音节是说话时最小的语言片断.单词中含有一个响亮音素的声音片断,就是一个音节.英语中的元音音素都是响亮音素,所以都是音节.一个元音音素就是一个音节,有几个元音音素就有几个音节.(请勿混淆元音音素和元音字母).例如: lake [leik] 是重读开音节, 单音节词.这个单词里有两个元音字母.e 不发音, 元音字母 a 读其字母的名称音 [ei].
	只有一个元音音素的单词是单音节词;有两个元音音素的单词是双音节词;有三个以上元音音素的单词就是多音节词.
	单独一个元音也能构成一个音节,例如: I [ai], a [ei] 等.
	元音音素是构成音节的最基本要素,而辅音音素就不能构成音节.但辅音音素 [l m n] 在词尾时,可以和它前面的辅音音素构成成音节, 是非重读音节, 例如: little [ˈlitl] .
重读符号	" ˈ " 是重读符号,重读符号在单音节词中全部省略,因为单音节词都是重读音节.重读符号只用于双音节词和多音节词中. (在双音节词中,一个是重读音节, 另一个是非重读音节.重读音节的词要用重读符号表示.), 例如: unit [ˈjuːnit] .
	在多音节词中,例如: 三个音节的词,有一个是重读音节,两个是非重读音节, 如: hospital [ˈhɔspitəl]; 四个音节的词, 有一个是重读音节, 有三个是非重读节,如 community [kəˈmjuːniti]; 五个音节的词, 有一个是重读音节, 一个是次重读音节, 三个是非重读音节, 如 university [juːniˈvəːsiti].

音节的划分规则:

单音节词的音节划分	有一个元音音素的英语单词就是单音节词, 单音节词都是重读音节. 重读符号在单音节词中全部省略.

单音节词的五大读音规则

重读开音节		重读闭音节		重读 R 音节		重读 Re 音节		重读字母组合	
a	name	a	tap	ar	car	are	hare	ay	bay
[ei]	[neim]	[æ]	[tæp]	[ɑ:]	[kɑ:]	[ɛə]	[hɛə]	[ei]	[bei]

实践练习

问: I 是五种读音规则中的哪一种?	答: 重读开音节, 单音节词, 读音是 [ai].
问: name 是五种读音规则中的哪一种?	答: 重读开音节, 单音节词, 读音是 [neim]. (划分音节取决于元音音素, 而不取决于元音字母. name 是重读开音节词, 虽然有两个元音字母, 但是 name 中的元音字母 e 不发音, 元音字母 a 读其字母的名称音 [ei]. 因此 name 还是单音节词, 读 [neim]).
问: tap 是五种读音规则中的哪一种?	答: 重读闭音节, 单音节词, 读音是 [tæp].
问: car 是五种读音规则中的哪一种?	答: 重读 R 音节, 单音节词, 读音是 [kɑ:].
问: hare 是五种读音规则中的哪一种?	答: 重读 Re 音节, 单音节词, 读音是 [hɛə].
问: bay 是五种读音规则中的哪一种?	答: 重读音节字母组合, 单音节词, 读音是 [bei]. (划分音节取决于元音音素, 而不取决于元音字母. bay 中有两个元音字母, 因为这个单词中 ay 是重读音节元音字母组合, 所以元音字母 a 和元音字母 y 不能分开, 只读一个音素 [ei]. 因此, bay 还是单音节词, 读 [bei]).

问：our 是五种读音规则中的哪一种？	答：重读音节字母组合，单音节词，读音是 [auə] (划分音节取决于元音音素，而不取决于元音字母. our 中有两个元音字母，因为这个单词中的 our 是元-辅音字母组合，所以元音字母. 和元音字母 u 以及辅音字母 r 不能分开，只读一个音素 [auə]，因此 our 还是单音节词.) 请注意：[auə] 音素是三合元音，在五十年代和六十年代出版的英语书中国际音标有 52 个.除了本书讲的 48 个国际音标外，还有一个双元音 [ɔə] 和三个三合元音 [auə], [aiə] 和 [ɔiə]. 因此, 这些三合元音都各自算作一个音素.

三合元音	例			词		
[aiə]	hour	[auə]	小时	our	[auə]	我们的
[aiə]	fire	[faiə]	火	quiet	[kwaiət]	安静的
[ɔiə]	loyal	[lɔiəl]	忠诚的	royal	[rɔiəl]	皇家

规则的双音词的音节划分	规则的双音节词的重读音节通常都在第一个音节，后一个音节是非重读音节.

	规则的双音节词的音节划分（常见的五种情况）
1.	在双音节词中，如果在发音的两个元音字母之间，只有一个辅音字母(r 除外)，该辅音字母属于后一个音节，例如：later（以后）和 solar（太阳的）. later 有两个元音字母 a 和 e，它们之间的辅音字母 t 属于后一个音节. 前边只剩下 la ,是单音节词，单音节词都是重读音节.这个词属于重读音节读音规则中的开音节读音，读 ['lei]. 后边的 ter 是非重读音节，要遵照非重读音节的读音规则. er 在非重读音节中读 [ə], ter 就读 [tə]. (非重读音节的读音规则在下文中详述) 所以 later 这个单词就读 ['leitə].
2.	在双音节词中，如果在发音的两个元音字母之间，有两个辅音字母(r 除外)，一个辅音字母属于前一个音节，另一个辅音字母属于后一个音节，例如：doctor（医生） 和 number（数字）. number 这个单词有两个元音字母 u 和 e，它们之间有两个辅音字母. 辅音字母 m 属于前一个音节，辅音字母 b 属于后一个音节，前一个音节 num 就是单音节词，单音节词都是重读音节. 这个词属于重读音节读音规则中的闭音节，读 ['nʌm]. 后一个音节 ber 是非重读音节，要参照非重读音节的读音规则读. er 在非重读音节中读 [ə], ber 就读 [bə], 所以 number 这个单词就读 ['nʌmbə].

3.	在双音节词中，如果在发音的两个元音字母之间，有辅音字母组合，ch, sh, th 等，它们不能分开，当作一个辅音字母看待，须划在一个音节内.例如: or<u>ch</u>ard（果园）和 por<u>tr</u>ait（肖像） or<u>ch</u>ard 这个单词有两个元音字母 o 和 a, 它们之间有三个辅音字母.在双音节词中，两个元音字母之间只能有两个辅音字母,那么这个单词中的三个辅音字母 rch 中必然有字母组合. ch 就是字母组合，因为字母组合不能分开，所以 ch 就算一个辅音字母，属于后一个音节，而 r 属于前一个音节. or 是单音节词，单音节词都是重读音节.这个词属于重读音节读音规则中的 R 音节，读 ['ɔː].后一个音节 <u>ch</u>ard 是非重读音节，要按照非重读音节的读音规则发音. ar 在非重读音节中读 [ə], <u>ch</u>ard 就读 [tʃəd]，所以, or<u>ch</u>ard 这个单词就读 ['ɔːtʃəd].
4.	在双音节词中，如果是双 R 音节，那么第一个音节中的重读 R 音节，要按照闭音节发音，例如: so<u>rr</u>y（对不起）和 ma<u>rr</u>y（结婚）. 在双音节词中，如果在发音的两个元音字母之间有两个 r 时，一个 r 属于前一音节，一个 r 属于后一音节，前一个音节 sor 就是单音节词，单音节词都是重读音节.这个词属于重读音节读音规则中的 R 音节，但是这个单词里有两个 r, 它是特殊的双 R 音节.在双 R 音节中的重读 R 音节，要按照闭音节发音,因此,sor 在此读 [sɔ].后一个音节 ry 是非重读音节，要按照非重读音节的读音规则发音.元音字母 y 在非重读音节中读 [i], ry 就读 [ri]，所以 sorry 这个单词就读 ['sɔri].

5.	元音音素是构成音节的最基本要素，辅音音素不能构成音节.但辅音音素 [l m n] 在词尾时，可以和它前面的辅音音素构成成音节，是非重读音节，例如:little ['litl]（小的）和 common ['kɔmn]（普通的）。 在双音节词中，如果在发音的两个元音字母之间有两个 r 时，一个 r 属于前一音节，一个 r 属于后一音节，前一个音节 sor 就是单音节词，单音节词都是重读音节.这个词属于重读音节读音规则中的 R 音节，但是这个单词里有两个r，它是特殊的双R音节.在双R音节中的重读R音节，要按照闭音节发音，因此,sor 在此读 ['sɔ]. 后一个音ry节是非重读音节，要按照非重读音节的读音规则发音.元音字母 y 在非重读音节中读 [i]， ry 就读 [ri]，所以 sorry 这个单词就读['sɔri].

不规则的双音节词的音节划分	不规则双音节词，重读音节在第二个音节上，第一个音节是非重读音节.

特殊情况是: 如果词首是 a, be, de, im, in, em, ma, re, to, com, con, dis, mis, pre 和 per 时，重读音节通常在后一个音节，非重读音节在第一个音节，例如: ago, before, decide, import, invite, employ, material, report, today, combine, construct, discard, mistake, prepare, perform 在 ago 这个单词中，词首 a 是非重读音节，a 就要按照非重读音节的读音规则发音. a 在非重读音节中读 [ə]. go 是单音节词，单音节词都是重读音节.这个词属于重读音节读音规则中的开音节,读 ['gəu]，所以, ago 这个单词就读 [ə'gəu].

第十七课　　　　练习
Lesson Seventeen　　Exercises

1.	什么是音节	
2.	重读符号用在哪儿	
3.	英语单音节词通常有几种读音规则	
4.	规则的双音节词的划分规则有几种	
5.	写出16个不规则的双音节词	
6.	朗读并抄写三合元音	

第十八课

重读音节和非重读音节	
重读音节	单音节词都是重读音节,所以重读符号在单音节词中全部省略.双音节词是含有两个元音音素的词,而这两个元音音素就是两个音节.这两个音节要有一个读得重些,一个读得轻些.读得重的音节就叫重读音节,读得轻的音节叫非重读音节.重读音节用重读符号 ['] 表示,重读符号 ['] 放在重读音节左上方,例如: unit [ˈjuːnit] (单位) 和 doctor [ˈdɔktə] (医生) 在 unit [ˈjuːnit] 这个双音节词中,在发音的两个元音字母 u 和 i 之间,只有一个辅音字母 n,该辅音字母 n 属于后一个音节.即:u 是一个音节,nit 是一个音节.那么前一个音节是重读音节,u 就是重读音节.这个词属于重读音节读音规则中的重读开音节,读 [juː].n-i-t 是非重读音节.辅音字母 n 和 t 在非重读音节中和在重读音节中的读音一样.而元音字母 i 要按照非重读音节的读音规则发音. i 在非重读音节中读 [i],所以 nit 就读 [nit],即 unit [ˈjuːnit].
非重读音节	辅音字母和辅音字母组合在非重读音节中的读音规则不变. 元音字母 a, o, u 在非重读音节中读 [ə] 元音字母 e, i, y 在非重读音节中读 [i]

元音字母在非重读音节中的规则的读音规则

元音字母	读音规则	例		词
A	[ə]	comma	central	ago
O		symbol	purpose	correct
U		album	campus	support
E	[i]	market	harvest	report
I		unit	notice	practice
Y		baby	party	happy

多音节词的划分规则	在多音节词中,重读音节通常在倒数第三个音节上. 例如: 倒数第三个音节就是重读音节,单音节词.是重读音节就有五种读音规则,此重读音节属于哪种重读读音规则的划分规则和双音节词的划分规则一样.

三个音节的词	有一个是重读音节,有两个是非重读音节.例如: hospital [ˈhɔspitl]（医院）

实践练习

问:	hospital 里有几个元音字母?	答:	三个. o, i, a
问:	重读音节在哪儿?	答:	在倒数第三个音节上
问:	o 和倒数第二个元音字母 i 间有几个辅音字母?	答:	有两个: s 和 p
问:	这两个辅音字母怎么划分?	答:	一个归前, 一个归后
问:	前面的 hos 是什么音节?	答:	闭音节. 读 [hɔs]
问:	闭音节是重读音节吗?	答:	是. 加重读符号 [ˈhɔs]
问:	元音字母 i 和 a 是什么音节?	答:	非重读音节.i 读 [i], a 读 [ə]
问:	辅音字母在非重读音节中有发音变化吗?	答:	没有. p 读 [p], t 读 [t], l 读 [l]
问:	hospital 怎么读?	答:	[ˈhɔspitəl] 是成音节, 读 [ˈhɔspitl]
四个音节的词	有一个是重读音节,有三个是非重读音节, 例如: community [kəˈmjuːniti]（社区）.		

实践练习

问:	Community 里有几个元音字母?	答:	四个: o, u, i, y
问:	重读音节在哪儿?	答:	在倒数第三个音节上: u

问:	u 和倒数第二个元音字母 i 间有几个辅音字母?	答:	有一个: n
问:	这个辅音字母怎么划分?	答:	一个辅音字母归后
问:	前面的 u 是什么音节?	答:	开音节,读 [ju:]
问:	开音节是重读音节吗?	答:	是. 加重读符号 [ˈju:]
问:	元音字母 i 和 y 是什么音节?	答:	非重读音节. i 读 [i], y 也读 [i]
问:	辅音字母在非重读音节中发音有变化吗?	答:	没有. n 读 [n], t 读 [t]
问:	u 是重读音节,那么最前边的. 是什么音节?	答:	非重读音节
问:	o 在非重读音节中读什么音?	答:	读 [ə]
问:	community 怎么读?	答:	[kəˈmju:niti]

五个音节的词	有一个是重读音节,一个是次重读音节,三个是非重读音节, 例如: university [ˌju:niˈvə:siti]（大学）

实践练习

问:	university 里有几个元音字母?	答:	五个: u, i, e, i, y
问:	重读音节在哪儿?	答:	在倒数第三个音节上: e
问:	e 和倒数第二个元音字母 i 间有几个辅音字母?	答:	有两个:r 和 s
问:	这两个辅音字母怎么划分?	答:	一个归前,一个归后
问:	前面的 ver 是什么音节?	答:	R 音节,读 [vә:]
问:	R 音节是重读音节吗?	答:	是. 加重读符号 ['vә:]
问:	元音字母 i 和 y 是什么音节?	答:	非重读音节. i 读 [i], y 也读 [i]
问:	现在倒数的三个音节怎么读?	答:	['vә:siti]
问:	e 是重读音节,e 开始再往前倒数第三个音节是什么音节?	答:	还是重读音节
问:	既然 u 又是重读音节了,那么 u 和 i 间有几个辅音字母?	答:	有一个: n
问:	这个辅音字母怎么划分?	答:	一个辅音字母归后
问:	前边的 u 是什么音节?	答:	开音节,读 [ju:]
问:	开音节是重读音节吗?	答:	是. 加重读符号
问:	前面已有重读符号了,这第二个重读符号怎么加呢?	答:	这种情况要在下边标次重读符 [ˌ]. 次重读也是重读,也要按重读音节的五大读音规则读,只是读时比第一个重读稍次点
问:	既然次重读也是重读,那么 u 后的 i 是什么音节?	答:	非重读音节
问:	那么 university 怎么读?	答:	[ˌju:ni'vә:siti]

第十八课 练习
Lesson Sixteen Exercises

1.	抄写元音字母在非重读音节中的规则的读音规则表 (抄写三遍)
2.	说一下辅音字母和辅音字母组合在非重读音节中的读音:
3.	写出 3 个三个音节的词并标出它们的音标
4.	写出 2 个四个音节的词并标出它们的音标
5.	写出 1 个五个音节的词并标出它们的音标

第十九课

元音字母在非重读音节中的不规则的读音规则

元音字母	发 音	例		词
a	[i]	passage	village	accurate
	[ei]	generate	separate	eliminate
	[ ]	hospital	digital	principal
o	[əu]	yellow	photo	also
	[ɔ]	population	dialogue	bookshop
	[ ]	pardon	button	cotton
u	[ju:]	popular	annual	accurate
	[u:]	February	century	usual
	[i]	minute		
e	[ə]	happen	camel	towel
i	[ai]	appetite	apologize	organize
	[ə]	festival	holiday	possible
y	[ai]	verify	qualify	modify

重读 Re 音节的特殊情况

在双音节或多音节词中，如果"一个元音字母 + r"之后还是元音字母，那么"一个元音字母 + r"通常也按 Re 音节读音．其读音规则如下：

重读 Re 音节的特殊情况	读 音	例		词
ar (+元音字母)	[ɛər]	various	vary	wary
or (+元音字母)	[ɔ: r]	story	glory	boring
ur (+元音字母)	[juər]	during	fury	durable
er (+元音字母)	[iər]	serious	material	experience
ir (+元音字母)	[aiər]	miry	spire	spiral

常用元音字母组合在非重读音节中的读音规则

元音字母组合	读音规则	例 词		
ai	[i]	curt<u>ai</u>n	cert<u>ai</u>n	
ay		birthd<u>ay</u>	Sund<u>ay</u>	Frid<u>ay</u>
ou	[ə]	nerv<u>ou</u>s	fam<u>ou</u>s	obvi<u>ou</u>s
ui	[i]	circ<u>ui</u>t	bisc<u>ui</u>t	
ee		coff<u>ee</u>	toff<u>ee</u>	
ei		forf<u>ei</u>t	surf<u>ei</u>t	forf<u>ei</u>ture
ey		donk<u>ey</u>	monk<u>ey</u>	

常用元,辅音字母组合在非重读音节中的读音规则

元,辅音字母组合	读音规则	例 词		
ar	[ə]	sol<u>ar</u>	coll<u>ar</u>	lun<u>ar</u>
or		doct<u>or</u>	tract<u>or</u>	mot<u>or</u>
ur		A<u>ur</u>burn		
er		lead<u>er</u>	writ<u>er</u>	winn<u>er</u>
our		lab<u>our</u>	col<u>our</u>	neighb<u>our</u>
ous		nerv<u>ous</u>	marvel<u>ous</u>	humor<u>ous</u>
ent	[ənt]	stud<u>ent</u>	presid<u>ent</u>	excell<u>ent</u>
ciou	[ʃə]	deli<u>ciou</u>s		
land	[lənd]	Fin<u>land</u>	Scot<u>land</u>	Is<u>land</u>
ture	[tʃə]	pic<u>ture</u>	na<u>ture</u>	lec<u>ture</u>
iture	[itʃə]	furn<u>iture</u>		
tion	[ʃən]	na<u>tion</u>	instruc<u>tion</u>	educa<u>tion</u>
ition	[iʃən]	pos<u>ition</u>	prepos<u>ition</u>	
stion	[stʃən]	que<u>stion</u>	sugge<u>stion</u>	
sion	[ʃən]	pen<u>sion</u>	exten<u>sion</u>	profes<u>sion</u>
sion	[ʒən]	occa<u>sion</u>	deci<u>sion</u>	colli<u>sion</u>
ision	[iʒən]	div<u>ision</u>	v<u>ision</u>	telev<u>ision</u>
tory	[tri]	fac<u>tory</u>	vic<u>tory</u>	labora<u>tory</u>

tary		secretary		
ment	[mənt]	payment	statement	basement
cial	[ʃəl]	special	artificial	social
sive	[siv]	expensive	explosive	passive
tive	[tiv]	active	effective	sensitive
cian	[ʃən]	technician	electrician	musician
tial	[ʃəl]	partial	martial	potential
sia	[ʃə]	Asia	Russia	Asian
tient	[ʃənt]	patient	patience	
sten	[sn]	listen	Christen	listen
stle	[sl]	whistle	castle	jostle
sure	[ʒə]	measure	pleasure	leisure
ther	[ðə]	weather	leather	brother
ful	[ful]	wonderful	beautiful	graceful
ist	[ist]	scientist	chemist	artist
mn	[m]	solemn	column	autumn

常用元,辅音字母组合在非重读音节中的读音规则 (特殊情况)

元,辅音字母组合	读音规则	例 词		
eer	[iə]	volunteer	engineer	pioneer
ier		cashier	premier	frontier
gu	[gw]	anguish	penguin	language
gu	[g]	guitar	guard	guess
gue		league	dialogue	logue
que	[k]	unique	boutique	cheque

第十九课　　　　　练习
Lesson Nineteen　　Exercises

1.	抄写元音字母在非重读音节中的不规则的读音规则表 (抄写一遍)
2.	抄写重读 Re 音节的特殊情况 (抄写三遍)
3.	抄写常用元音字母组合在非重读音节中的读音规则表 (抄写三遍)
4.	抄写常用元, 辅音字母组合在非重读音节中的读音规则 (抄写两遍)

第二十课　　　常用的音变现象

1.	辅音字母 t 读 [t]，但是如果它后面跟辅音字母 y 读 [j] 时，要产生音变现象(或同化现象).这时的辅音字母 t 不能读 [t]，而产生音变现象，要读 [tʃ]，然后与后边的 [j] 拼读成音.例如: Nice to meet you. 单词 Meet 中的辅音字母 t 读 [t]，它后面跟的单词 you 中的辅音字母 y 读 [j]. 这时的辅音字母 t 不能读 [t]，而产生了音变现象，要读 [tʃ]，然后与后边的[ju:]拼读成音. 练习: Not yet.　　　Courtyard　　First year　　What about you?
2.	辅音字母 d 读 [d]，但是如果它后面跟辅音字母 y 读 [j] 时，要产生音变现象（或同化现象）. 这时的辅音字母 d 不能读 [d]，而产生音变现象，要读 [dʒ]. 然后与后边的 [j] 拼读成音，例如: And you? And 中的辅音字母 d 读 [d]，它后面跟的单词 you 中的辅音字母 y 读 [j]. 这时的辅音字母 d 不能读 [d]，而产生了音变现象，要读 [dʒ]，然后与后边的[ju:]拼读成音. 练习: Second year　　　　　　　Could you do it again? 　　　Would you please help me ?
3.	辅音字母 "s" 发 [s] 音，但是，如果读 [j] 的辅音字母 "y" 在辅音字母 "s"后，辅音字母 "s"的发音有变化（前提条件是辅音字母 "y" 和辅音字母 "s" 必须在同一个意群内). 这时, 辅音字母 "s" 不能发 [s] 音，而要读 [ʃ] 音. 然后, [ʃ] 和 [j] 开头的单词相拼，例如: I miss you. 单词 "miss" 中"s"本来应该读 [s]，但是，由于读 [j] 的辅音字母 "y" 在辅音字母 "s"后，所以发音变化了. 辅音字母 "s" 不能发 [s] 音，而要读 [ʃ] 音. 然后, [ʃ] 和 [j] 开头的单词 "you" 相拼. 练习: I miss you badly.

4. 下列字母组合在单词中发音有变化

辅音字母组合	读 音	例		词	
teen	[ti:n]	thirteen	fourteen	fifteen	sixteen
in	[in]	inch	input	insect	inside
en	[en]	end	enter	entry	ten
an	[æn]	an	and	ant	fan
un	[ʌn]	under	undress	unless	bun
an	[ɑ:n]	answer	dance	lance	plant
on	[ɔn]	on	ongoing	onto	fond
oon	[u:n]	moon	noon	boon	soon
oun	[aun]	round	found	bound	pound

第二十课 练习
Lesson Twenty　　Exercises

1.	抄写并朗读下列练习	Not yet. Courtyard First year student
2.	抄写并朗读下列练习	Second year students Could you do it again? Dupond Would you please help me ?
3.	抄写并朗读下列练习	I miss you badly.
4.	抄写并朗读 9 个在单词中发音有变化的字母组合表	

第二十一课　S _ 辅音连缀

十种 S _ 辅音连缀

sl	[sl]	slap	sleep	slim	slip	slow
sm	[sm]	small	smart	smell	smile	smoke
sn	[sn]	snap	sneeze	snake	snow	sneak
sw	[sw]	sweep	sweet	swim	swear	swan
sc	[sk]	scar	scream	scab	scoop	scum
sk	[sk]	sketch	skill	skin	skinny	sky
sp	[sp]	spade	Spain	spread	spring	spy
sq	[sk]	square	squad	squall	squib	squirm
st	[st]	star	stay	step	stop	stuck
str	[str]	stream	street	stress	strike	strong

四种 S _ 辅音连缀是规则的情形

sl	[sl]	slap	sleep	slim	slip	slow
sm	[sm]	small	smart	smell	smile	smoke
sn	[sn]	snap	sneeze	snake	snow	sneak
sw	[sw]	sweep	sweet	swim	swear	swap

六种 S _ 辅音连缀是不规则的情形

sc	[sk]	scar	scream	scab	scoop	scum
sk	[sk]	sketch	skill	skin	skinny	sky
sp	[sp]	spade	Spain	spread	spring	spy
sq	[sk]	square	squad	squall	squib	squirm
st	[st]	star	stay	step	stop	stuck
str	[str]	stream	street	stress	strike	strong

例：辅音连缀 sc_ 中的 S _
sc_ 辅音连缀中的辅音字母"s"发［s］音. 在辅音字母"s"后的 sc_ 辅音连缀中的辅音字母"c", 已经产生了浊化现象. 也就是说, 辅音字母"s"后的辅音字母"c"不能发清辅音[k], 而要发浊辅音［g］.（注意：虽然"scar"发［skɑ:］音. 但是, 音素要照写, 不能改变.）
例：辅音连缀 sk_ 中的 S _
sk_ 辅音连缀中的辅音字母"s"发［s］音. 在辅音字母"s"后 sk_ 辅音连缀中的辅音字母"k", 已经产生了浊化现象. 也就是说, 辅音字母"s"后的辅音字母"k"不能发清辅音［k］, 而要发浊辅音［g］.（注意：虽然"sky"发［skai］音. 但是, 音素要照写, 不能改变.）
例：辅音连缀 sp_ 中的 S _
sp_ 辅音连缀中的辅音字母"s"发［s］音. 在辅音字母"s"后的 sp_ 辅音连缀中的辅音字母"p", 已经产生了浊化现象. 也就是说, 辅音字母"s"后的辅音字母"p"不能发清辅音［p］, 而要发浊辅音［b］.（注意：虽然"spy"发［spai］音. 但是, 音素要照写, 不能改变.）
例：辅音连缀 sq_ 中的 S _
sq_ 辅音连缀中的辅音字母"s"发［s］音. 在辅音字母"s"后的 sq_ 辅音连缀中的辅音字母"q", 已经产生了浊化现象. 也就是说, 辅音字母"s"后的辅音字母"q"不能发清辅音［k］, 而要发浊辅音［g］.（注意：虽然"square"发［skwεə］音. 但是, 音素要照写, 不能改变.）
例：辅音连缀 st_ 中的 S _
st_ 辅音连缀中的辅音字母"s"发［s］音. 在辅音字母"s"后的 st_ 辅音连缀中的辅音字母"t", 已经产生了浊化现象. 也就是说, 辅音字母"s"后的辅音字母"t"不能发清辅音［t］, 而要发浊辅音［d］.（注意：虽然"star"发［stɑ:］音. 但是, 音素要照写, 不能改变.）
例：辅音连缀 str_ 中的 S _
str_ 辅音连缀中的辅音字母"s"发［s］音. 在辅音字母"s"后的 str_ 辅音连缀中的辅音字母"tr", 已经产生了浊化现象. 也就是说, 辅音字母"s"后的辅音字母"tr"不能发清辅音[tr], 而要发浊辅音［dr］.（注意：虽然"street"发［stri:t］音. 但是, 音素要照写, 不能改变.）

如果不是辅音连缀"sc, sk, sp, sq, st 和 str"开头的单词中的"S _"辅音连缀，一切按正常情况读音。

浊化：	辅音字母 s 读 [s]，它后面的清辅音要产生浊化现象。即：辅音字母 s 后的清辅音要按浊辅音读。例如:
1.	spend [spend] 中 [s] 后面的清辅音 [p] 要产生浊化现象。即要按浊辅音 [b] 读.（注意：虽然 spend 读 [sbend]，但是音标还要写成 [spend]）
2.	star [stɑ:] 中 [s] 后面的清辅音 [t] 要产生浊化现象。即要按浊辅音 [d] 读.（注意：虽然 star 读 [sdɑ:]，但是音标还要写成 [stɑ:]）
3.	sky [skai] 中 [s] 后面的清辅音 [k] 要产生浊化现象。即要按浊辅音 [g] 读.（注意：虽然 sky 读 [sgai]，但是音标还要写成 [skai]）
4.	square [skwεə] 中 [s] 后面的清辅音 [k] 要产生浊化现象。即要按浊辅音 [g] 读.（注意：虽然 square 读 [sgwεə]，但是音标还要写成 [skwεə]）
5.	street [stri:t] 中 [s] 后面的清辅音 [tr] 要产生浊化现象。即要按浊辅音 [dr] 读.（注意：虽然 street 读 [sdri:t]，但是音标还要写成 [stri:t]）

English Pronunciation for Chinese Speakers

第二十一课　　　　练习
Lesson Twenry-one　　Exercises

1.	抄写 S _ 辅音连缀的 10 种情况: (抄写一遍)

2.	抄写四种规则的 S _ 辅音连缀表: (抄写一遍)

3.	抄写六种不规则的 S _ 辅音连缀表: (抄写一遍)

第二十二课

常 用 的 连 读 现 象		
第一种现象	在同一个意群中,如果相邻两词中的前一个词以辅音音素结尾,后一个词是以元音音素开头,在说话或朗读句子时,习惯上很自然地将辅音音素与元音音素拼起来连读,这种语音现象叫连读. 例如: I like it very much. like [laik] 中的 [k] 是辅音音素, [it] 中的 [i] 是元音音素,辅音音素 [k] 拼元音音素 [i] 的现象就是连读现象.
第二种现象	在同一个意群中,如果前一个词是以-r 或者-re 结尾,后一个词是以元音音素开头,这时的 r 或 re 不但要发辅音音素[r] 音,而且还要与后面的元音音素拼起来连读. 这种语音现象叫连读. 例如: See you later on. later [ˈleitə] 这个单词是以 r 结尾,后一个单词 on [ɔn] 是以元音音素 [ɔ] 开头,这时的 r 不但要发辅音音素 [r] 音,而且还要与后面的元音音素 [ɔ] 拼起来连读. 因此, later on 要读作 [ˈleitər ɔn].

| 第二十二课 | | 练习 |
| Lesson Twenty-two | | Exercises |

1.	常用的连读现象有几种	
2.	抄写并朗读下列练习	I like it very much.
3.	抄写并朗读下列练习	See you later on.

第二十三课

	爆 破 音
爆破音的失去爆破或不完全爆破通常有	1. 爆破音后跟爆破音　爆破音失去爆破并不是完全失去爆破,而是憋住一口气,只做发爆破音的姿势(但不能发出爆破音),做瞬间停顿,然后直接发它后面跟的爆破音. 例如: He writes with his red pen. red [red] 中的 [d] 是爆破音,但不完全爆破.要憋住一口气,只做发爆破音 [d] 的姿势(但不能发出爆破音),做瞬间停顿,然后直接发它后面跟的爆破音[p]就可以了.
	2. 爆破音在词尾　爆破音在词尾要失去爆破, 要憋住一口气,做发爆破音的姿势 (但不能发出爆破音),做瞬间停顿,然后发出轻声的爆破音 [b, p, t, d, k, g] 就可以了, 例如: That's my hat. hat [hæt] 中的 [t] 是爆破音,但失去爆破. 要憋住一口气,只做发爆破音 [t] 的姿势 (但不能发出爆破音),做瞬间停顿, 然后发出轻声的爆破音 [t] 就可以了.
	3. 爆破音在词首或元音前　爆破音在词首或元音前,要不完全爆破, 需憋住一口气,做发爆破音的姿势 (但不能发出爆破音),做瞬间停顿,然后和后面的元音相拼就可以了, 例如: I play basketball in the morning. play [plei] 中的 [p] 是在词首的爆破音,要不完全爆破,需憋住一口气,做发爆破音的姿势 (但不能发出爆破音), 做瞬间停顿,然后读后面的辅音就可以了. 而 basketball 中的 [b] 是在元音前的爆破音,要不完全爆破. 需憋住一口气,做发爆破音的姿势(但不能发出爆破音), 做瞬间停顿,然后和后面的元音相拼就可以了.

第二十三课 练习
Lesson Twenty-three Exercises

1.	通常爆破音有几种情况	
2.	抄写并朗读下列练习	He writes with his red pen.
3.	抄写并朗读下列练习	That's my hat.
4.	抄写并朗读下列练习	I play basketball in the morning.

第二十四课

实词和功能词的读音规则	一般地说，实词重读，功能词非重读. 但是，功能词在强调时(通常在句首或句尾)，需要重读.
实词包括	名词, 数词, 形容词, 副词和行为动词
功能词包括	介词, 冠词, 连词, 代词, 联系动词, 助动词和情态动词
感叹词	属于独立成分
例如：	A: Where are you from?　　　　B: I'm from Canada. Where are you from? from 是介词, 虽然属于功能词. 但是此单词在词尾,所以属于强调. 既然属于强调,就要重读. from 中的元音字母 o 是重读闭音节, 读 [ɔ], 因此 from 读 [frɔm]. I'm from Canada from 是介词, 属于功能词. 要非重读, from 中的元音字母 o 在非重读音节中读[ə], 因此 from 读 [frəm].

第二十四课　　　　练习
Lesson Twenty-four　　Exercises

1.	实词的读音规则是什么	
2.	功能词的读音规则是什么	

第二十五课

停 顿 与 意 群	
停顿	通常停顿只发生在长句子里.要想读准，读好任何一个长句子，就一定要懂得长句子的停顿，因为有的长句子，不可能一口气读完，这就需要停顿下来，换口气再读. 这个过程就是停顿.但是，英语中的停顿是有规律的，那就是停顿只能停顿在一个意群之后，如果停顿在错误的地方，就会使对话给对方造成误解.
意群	意群就是在一个句子中按意思或结构分出的各个句子成分，一个句子成分就是一个意群. 因此，意群可以是一个单词，也可以是一个词组或一个从句. 例如: I'd like to learn the pausing very much. 这句话里有 4 个意群,即: 有 4 个停顿.
要想读准英语的任何一个长句子,必须要掌握好停顿和意群. 要想读好英语的任何一个长句子，还必须还要掌握好英语的节奏.关于英语的节奏，请见下节.	

English Pronunciation for Chinese Speakers

第二十五课　　　　练习
Lesson Twenty-five　　Exercises

1.	停顿的原则是什么	
2.	意群的定义是什么	

第二十六课

英语的节奏	英语是一种重读音节的语言. 重读音节就是英语中的每句话的基本要素(即英语中的每句话里必须至少有一个重读音节). 英语中的每句话的节奏都是由句中的重读音节的多少来决定的. 英语是一种有节奏感的语言. 对于把英语作为第二语言的中国人来说, 说英语恰似唱歌, 而歌曲的节奏又恰似宁静的山涧小溪的流水. 如果掌握了英语的节奏, 会让说英语的人感到是一种自我享受和自我陶冶, 也会让听英语的人感到是一种陶冶情操的享受和心旷神怡的欣赏. 优美的英语语言就体现在它具有强烈的犹如轻音乐般的节奏感和恰似宁静的山涧小溪流水的语调上. 怎么样才能掌握英语的节奏呢?
掌握节奏的技巧	● 读单词中的每个音素要精确清楚; ● 句中的音变现象要符合英语习惯; ● 一句话的停顿要恰到好处(停顿一定要在意群之间进行); ● 一句话的意群要准确无误; ● 说话的语调要恰似宁静的山涧小溪流水(读升调要升在一句话的最后的一个单词的最后一个音节上. 读降调也要降在一句话的最后的一个单词的最后一个音节上, 绝不要把英语读得像黄河的流水那样汹涌澎湃)

English Pronunciation for Chinese Speakers

第二十六课　　　　　练习
Lesson Twenty-six　　Exercises

1.	英语是什么样的语言	
2.	怎么样掌握英语的节奏	

第二十七课　　　语调

语调	英语的语调是很复杂的. 对于我们学习基础英语的学生们只要了解语调的基础调 --- 升调和降调就可以了.

升　　调

英语的升调怎么升？	英语的升调要升在单词的最后一个音节上. 例如: party 的升调要升在单词 party 的最后一个音节[i]上. 例如: Are you feeling cold？升调要升在句子的最后一个单词 cold 的最后一个音节[əu]上.
何时用升调	何时用升调: 英语中的一般疑问句, 选择疑问句, 反意疑问句用升调.

中国学生学好升调的窍门

把普通话拼音中的二声当成升调, 四声当成降调. 例如: 把单词 fee [fi:] 读成升调. fee 在普通话中有四个音. 飞, 肥, 匪, 费. （肥是升调, 费是降调.）"肥"就是我们要读的升调. 其它英语单词的升调练习方法, 以此类推.

何时用升调

1.	一般疑问句句末单词的最后一个音节用升调：例如：Do you study English？中最后那个单词 English 中的最后一个音节 [i] 用升调
2.	选择疑问句中 or 前的那个单词的最后一个音节用升调.例如：Is she beautiful or ugly？中 or 前 beautiful 中的最后一个音节 [u] 用升调.
3.	反意疑问句句末那个单词的最后一个音节用升调，例如：It's a very lovely day, isn't it？中最后那个单词 it 中的最后一个音节 [i] 用升调.

除上述情况外,用升调的其它场合

1.	读人名的每个字母时,最后一个字母读降调,前边的字母都用升调，例如：人名 John 中的 J – o – h 读升调, n 读降调.
2.	数词通常读升调,例如:查数时:如果数 5 个数字, 前 4 个数字 one, two, three, four 用升调, 最后一个数字 5 用降调; 读电话号时,最后一个号读降调，前边的号都用升调, 例如:电话号 (416) 888-9166 中的 4-1-6-8-8-8-9-1-6 读升调,最后一个号码 6 读降调.
3.	并列连词前的那个单词的最后一个音节用升调，例如：Tea or coffee？中的 tea 读升调.
4.	英语句子中有并列关系的单词和句子用升调，例如：I like apple, orange, pine apple, banana and so on. 中的 apple, orange, pine apple, banana 用升调.
5.	A: Do you play piano every evening? B: Sometimes I do. Sometimes I don't. 上述对话中的第一句 "Sometimes I do." 用升调说.
6.	主句在后, 状语从句或状语在前, 该状语从句或状语的最后一个单词的最后一个音节用升调：例如：At 07:00 in the evening, the basketball match began. 中的 At 07:00 in the evening 用升调.
7.	通常英语的特殊疑问句句末要用降调,但是引导特殊疑问句的 9 个疑问词中的 7 个疑问词 who, which, what, how, when, where, why 以及部分疑问词组 what time 等有时也可以用升调，但是用升调和用降调

	的意思是不一样的，例如: A: The Christmas Party will start at 11:50 am.　B: What time?　A: At 11:50 am. 上述对话中的B用升调说"What time?"，其意思是没有听清楚对方说话中的某一部分，而希望对方把没有听清楚对方说话中的那部分再说一遍。
8.	B: What's that?　A: Would you please go to the principal's office after school? 上述对话中的B用升调说"What's that?"，其意思是没有听清楚对方说话中的某一部分，而希望对方把没有听清楚对方说话中的那部分再说一遍。
9.	通常英语的陈述句句末要用降调，但是有时也可以用升调，例如: He won't come tomorrow, I'm afraid. 陈述句 I'm afraid 用升调表示怀疑。
10	A: I'm sorry to trouble you. B: That's O. K.　(or That's all right)　上述对话中B用升调说"That's O. K. (or That's all right)"的意思是没有关系。
11.	A: Linda said she will fill out the form for me.　B: There you go! You won't look for a translator. 上述对话中B用升调说"There you go!"是用在结束一段对话时用的。
12.	A: Is it b-o-s-s ? B: That's right. 上述对话中B用升调说"That's right."的意思是你说对了。
13.	A: Excuse me. B: Yes ? 上述对话中B用升调说"Yes?"的意思是"什么事呀？"
14.	A: My phone number is (416) 888-9166　B: Sorry? 上述对话中B用升调说"Sorry？"的意思是"对不起,我没听清,请再说一遍"
15.	A: P-e-t-e-r B: Pardon ? (or Pardon me?/I beg your pardon?) 上述对话中B用升调说"Pardon？的意思是"对不起,我没听清,请再说一遍"。

English Pronunciation for Chinese Speakers

第二十七课　　　　　练习
Lesson Twenty-seven　　Exercises

1.	英语的升调怎么升	
2.	何时用升调	

第二十八课　　　降调

英语的降调怎么降	1. 英语的降调要降在单词的最后一个音节上，例如：remember 的降调要降在最后一个音节 er [ə] 上. 2. 英语的降调要降在句子的最后一个单词的最后一个音节上，例如: We go to school every day. 降调要降在句子的最后一个单词 day 的最后一个音节[ei]上.
何时用降调	英语的陈述句, 祈使句, 感叹句和特殊疑问句用降调.

何时用降调

1.	陈述句用降调, 例如: We learn English in the LINC school every day. 中最后的单词 day 中的最后一个音节 [ei] 用降调.
2.	祈使句用降调, 例如: Open your books at page eight. 中最后的单词 eight 中的最后一个音节 [ei] 用降调.
3.	感叹句用降调, 例如: What a beautiful day it is ! 中最后的单词 is 中的最后一个音节 [i] 用降调.
4.	特殊疑问句用降调, 例如: Where are you from? 中最后的单词 from 中的最后一个音节 [ɔ] 用降调.

除上述情况外,用降调的其它场合

1.	Oh! It's almost 10:30 am. Isn't your brother going late to the air port ! 句子 Isn't your brother going late to the air port ! 在形式上是否定结构的一般疑问句,但是它实际上是个感叹句.既然是感叹句,那么, 这个句子的最后那个单词 port 的最后那个音节 [ɔ:] 就要用降调.

2.	You want to earn money, aren't you? 反意疑问句句末用升调表示疑问.反意疑问句句末用降调表示加强语气. 这句话如要表示加强语气, 它最后那个单词 you 的最后那个音节 [ju:] 就要用降调.
3.	英语讲话或讲稿中的 Firstly (第一), Secondly (第二), Thirdly (第三) 等顺序词应用降调.
4.	除上述讲的用升调情况外, 就都是用降调的.

辅音字母和辅音字母组合发音的特殊情况:

特 殊 情 况	读 音	例 词			
b 在词尾, 前有 m 时	不发音	bomb	lamb	thumb	
				tomb	
h 在 ex 和 R r 后		exhibition	exhausted		rhyme
h 在词尾		Ah	Oh	myrrh	Sarah
k 在词首, 后跟 n 时		knife	knee	kneel	knead
l 在下列词中		palm	calm	talk	walk
m 在单词中辅音字母 n 前		mnemonic		mnemonics	
n 在非重读音节词中 m 后		Autumn		column	
p 在词首, 后跟 n 时		pneumonia		pneumatic	
p 在词首, 后跟 s 时		psaltery		psychic	
p 在词首, 后跟 t 时		ptarmigan		pterodactyl	
t 在词尾字母组合 -sten 中		fasten		listen	
t 在词尾字母组合 -stle 中		castle		whistle	
疑问副词或其它情况中的 wh 开头的词	h 不发音	What	when	where	whale
疑问代词和另外 8.个单词中的 wh 开头的词	w 不发音	who	whose	whom	who-ever
		whole	whole-sale		wholly
wr 开头的单词中的	w 不发音	wrong	write		wrist

		science	scissors	excited
c 在 S s 和 X x 后	不发音			
e, i 在 g 前读	[g]	gear	get gift	gill girl
形容词的比较级或最高级中的 ng	[ŋg]	long	longer	longest
ng 的后有 er 或 le 结尾的单词		young	younger	youngest
		finger	anger single	mingle
nge 结尾的单词	[ndʒ]	change	strange	arrange

重读音节元音字母组合和重读音节元,辅音字母组合在单词中的读音特殊情况

元音字母组合和元,辅音字母组合	读 音	例 词		
ua	[wa:]	suave	guano	
ue	[u:]	blue	true	glue
ue	[ju:]	due	cue	sue
ui	[u:]	cruise	bruise	sluice
ui	[ju:]	nuisance	suit	
ui	[ju:i]	tuition	suicide	suicidal
ui	[u:i]	fluid	ruin	
ui	[wi]	cuirass	cuisine	squid
ui	[i]	build	guild	guitar
ui	[ai]	guide	guidance	guise
eo	[iə]	theory	peony	peon
eu	[ju:]	feud	deuce	neuter
eu	[iə]	geum		
ia	[aiə]	dial	dialogue	diabetes
io	[aiə]	lion	pioneer	violin
eir	[iə]	their	weird	heir
ier		fierce	pier	bier

常用元音字母组合在非重读音节中的读音规则 (特殊情况)

元音字母组合	读 音	例		词
ia	[iə]	Victoria	Julia	Maria
ie	[i]	movie	cookie	Loonie
io	[iə]	million	union	onion
iu		medium	auditorium	stadium

第二十八课　　　　　练习
Lesson Twenty-eight　　Exercises

1.	英语的降调怎么降	
2.	何时用降调	

英语元音音素发音说明

1. [i:] 前元音	
前元音, 即舌前部（舌尖）活动. [i:] 音与普通话中的"一"音相似, 但不相同. 发 [i:] 音时, 音要发得长点, 因为有长音符号. [i:] 是长元音. 发音结束时, 舌尖仍然抵住下牙齿.	
发音三要素	1. 唇势: 最扁　　　　2. 齿距: 几乎闭合 3. 舌位: 舌尖抵紧下牙齿

2. [i] 前元音	
前元音, 即舌前部(舌尖) 活动. [i] 音是元音字母 A a 的尾音. 不要发成普通话中的"一"音, 因为"一"音太长, 而 [i] 音是短元音. [i] 音是 [ei] 音的尾音, 并不是 [i:] 音的短音. 发音结束时,舌尖仍然抵住下牙齿.	
发音三要素	1. 唇势: 扁　　　　　2. 齿距: 半个扁指 3. 舌位: 舌尖抵紧下牙齿

3. [e] 前元音	
前元音, 即舌前部 (舌尖) 活动. [e] 音与普通话中的"艾"音相似,但不相同. 普通话中的"艾"音太长, 而前元音 [e] 音是短元音. 发音结束时, 舌尖仍然抵住下牙齿.	
发音三要素	1. 唇势: 扁　　　　　2. 齿距: 一个扁指 3. 舌位: 舌尖抵紧下牙齿

4. [æ] 前元音	
前元音, 即舌前部活动. 舌前部就是舌尖. [æ] 音与普通话中的"碍"音相似, 但不相同. 普通话中的"碍"音太长, 而前元音 [æ] 音是短元音. 在发音结束时, 舌尖仍然抵住下牙齿.	
发音三要素	1. 唇势: 扁　　　　　2. 齿距: 两个扁指 3. 舌位: 舌尖抵紧下牙齿

5. [ʌ] 中元音	
中元音, 即舌中部（舌端）活动. [ʌ] 音与普通话中的"呵"音相似, 但不相同. 普通话中的"呵"音太长, 开口太大, 而中元音 [ʌ] 音是短元音. 发音结束时, 仍然保持原来的口型, 不要闭嘴.	
发音三要素	1. 唇势: 扁　　　　2. 齿距: 两个扁指 3. 舌位: 舌头平伸于口中, 舌前部不要碰到上齿和下齿, 舌中部在发音时抬高

6. [ə] 中元音	
中元音, 即舌中部（舌端）活动. [ə] 音与普通话中的"阿"音相似, 但不相同. 普通话中的"阿"音太长, 开口太大, 而中元音 [ə] 音是短元音. 发音结束时, 仍然保持原来的口型, 不要闭嘴.	
发音三要素	1. 唇势: 扁　　　　2. 齿距: 两个扁指 3. 舌位: 舌头平伸于口中, 舌前部不要碰到上齿和下齿, 舌中部在发音时抬高

7. [ə:] 中元音	
中元音, 即舌中部（舌端）活动. [ə:] 音与普通话中"饿"音相似, 但不相同. 普通话中的"饿"音太放松, 而发中元音[ə:]音时, 口腔稍紧张. [ə:]是长元音, 发音结束时, 仍然保持原来的口型, 不要闭嘴.	
发音三要素	1. 唇势: 扁　　　　2. 齿距: 两个扁指 3. 舌位: 舌头平伸于口中, 舌前部不要碰到上齿和下齿, 舌中部在发音时抬高.

8. [ɑ:] 后元音	
后元音, 即舌后部(舌根)活动. [ɑ:] 音与普通话中的"啊"音相似, 但不相同. 普通话中的"啊"音太放松, 而发后元音 [ɑ:] 音时, 口全开, 舌头平伸于口中. 舌前部和舌中部都不要碰到上齿和下齿, 舌后部要下压. [ɑ:] 是长元音, 发音结束时, 仍然保持原来的口型, 不要闭嘴.	

发音三要素	1. 唇势: 口全开 1. 椭圆形　　2. 齿距: 三个扁指 3. 舌位: 舌头平伸于口中, 舌前部和舌中部都不要碰到上齿和下齿, 发音时舌后部下压.

9. [ɔ] 后元音

后元音, 即舌后部(舌根)活动. [ɔ]音与普通话中的"凹"音相似, 但不相同. 普通话中的"凹"音太放松, 而发后元音[ɔ]音时, 口是大圆形, 舌头平伸于口中, 舌前部和舌中部都不要碰到上齿和下齿, 舌后部要下压, 尽量要向外放音. [ɔ]是短元音. 发音结束时, 仍然保持原来的口型, 不要闭嘴.

发音三要素	1. 唇势: 大圆形　　2. 齿距: 两个半扁指 3. 舌位: 舌头平伸于口中, 舌前部和舌中部都不要碰到上齿和下齿, 发音时舌后部下压.

10. [ɔː] 后元音

后元音, 即舌后部(舌根)活动. [ɔː]音与普通话中的"奥"音相似, 但不相同. 普通话中的"奥"音太放松, 而发后元音[ɔː]音时, 口是大圆形, 舌头平伸于口中, 舌前部和舌中部都不要碰到上齿和下齿, 舌后部要下压, 尽量要向外放音. [ɔː]是长元音. 发音结束时, 仍然保持原来的口型, 不要闭嘴.

发音三要素	1. 唇势: 大圆形　　2. 齿距: 两个半扁指 3. 舌位: 舌头平伸于口中, 舌前部和舌中部都不要碰到上齿和下齿, 发音时舌后部下压

11. [u] 后元音

后元音, 即舌后部(舌根)活动. [u]音与普通话中的"屋"音相似, 但不相同. 普通话中的"屋"音太放松, 而发后元音[u]音时, 口是小圆形, 舌头平伸于口中, 舌前部和舌中部都不要碰到上齿和下齿. 发音时, 舌后部要上抬, 尽量要向里拢音. [u]是短元音, 发音结束时, 仍然保持原来的口型, 不要闭嘴.

发音三要素	1. 唇势：小圆形　　2. 齿距：一个半扁指
	3. 舌位：舌头平伸于口中，舌前部和舌中部都不要碰到上齿和下齿，发音时舌后部上抬

12. [u:] 后元音	
后元音，即舌后部（舌根）活动. [u:] 音与普通话中的"务"音相似，但不相同. 普通话中的"务"音太放松，而发后元音 [u:] 音时，口是小圆形. 舌头平伸于口中，舌前部和舌中部都不要碰到上齿和下齿. 发音时，舌后部要上抬，尽量要向里拢音. [u:] 是长元音. 发音结束时，仍然保持原来的口型，不要闭嘴.	
发音三要素	1. 唇势：口是小圆形　　2. 齿距：一个半扁指
	3. 舌位：舌头平伸于口中. 舌前部和舌中部都不要碰到上齿和下齿，发音时舌后部上抬

13. [e i] 合口双元音	
合口双元音 [e i] 是由第一个元音 [e] 向第二个元音 [i] 滑动发音时，嘴型一定要从大到小滑动. [e i] 音与普通话拼音中的"ei"音相似，但不相同. 普通话拼音中的"ei"音太放松，嘴型大，且没有滑动. 而发合口双元音 [e i] 音时，由第一个元音 [e] 向第二个元音 [i] 滑动，嘴型一定要从大到小滑动，才能发出合口双元音 [e i] 音. 发音结束时，舌尖仍然抵下牙齿，不要闭嘴.	
发音三要素	1. 唇势：扁　　2. 齿距：从一个扁指滑动到半个扁指
	3. 舌位：舌前部紧抵下齿

14. [ai] 合口双元音

合口双元音 [ai] 是由第一个元音 [a] 向第二个元音 [i] 滑动发音时，嘴型一定要从大到小滑动. [ai] 音与普通话拼音中的"啊"和合口双元音 [ei] 的第二个元音 [i] 的发音相似，但不相同.普通话拼音中的"啊"音太放松，而发合口双元音中的 [a] 音时,口全开，舌下压. 因此, 发合口双元音 [ai] 音时,要由第一个元音 [a] 向第二个元音[i]滑动，嘴型一定要从大到小滑动，才能发出合口双元音 [ai] 音. 发音结束时，舌尖仍然抵下牙齿，不要闭嘴.

发音三要素	1. 唇势: 嘴型从口全开滑动到很扁 2. 齿距: 从三个扁指滑动到半个扁指 3. 舌位: 从舌后部活动滑动到舌前部，发音后，以舌尖紧抵下牙齿结束发音

15. [au] 合口双元音

合口双元音 [au] 是由第一个元音 [a] 向第二个元音 [u] 滑动发音时，嘴型一定要从大到小滑动. [au] 音与普通话拼音中的"啊"和后元音 [u] 音相似，但不相同.普通话拼音中的"啊"音太放松，而合口双元音中的[a]音时，口全开，舌下压. 发音结束时，嘴型是小圆.

发音三要素	1. 唇势: 嘴型从口全开滑动到小圆 2. 齿距: 从三个扁指滑动到一个半个扁指 3. 舌位: 发音时，舌后部从下压放音滑动到舌后部上拢音.以唇势: 小圆, 齿距: 一个半扁指, 舌位: 后部上抬拢音结束发音

16. [əu] 合口双元音

合口双元音 [əu] 是由第一个元音 [ə]向第二个元音 [u] 滑动发音时，嘴型一定要从大到小滑动. [əu]音与普通话拼音中的"沤"音相似，但不相同. 普通话拼音中的"沤"音只有一个音，而发合口双元音 [əu] 音时，要由第一个元音[ə]向第二个元音 [u] 音滑动，嘴型一定要从大到小滑动，才能发出合口双元音 [əu] 音. 发音结束时，嘴型是小圆.

发音三要素	1. 唇势: 嘴型从扁到小圆
	2. 齿距: 从两个扁指滑动到一个半个扁指
	3. 舌位: 发音时,从舌中部滑动到舌后部上抬拢音. 以唇势: 小圆, 齿距: 一个半个扁指, 舌位: 舌后部上抬拢音结束发音.

17. [ɔi] 合口双元音

合口双元音 [ɔi] 是由第一个元音 [ɔ] 向第二个元音 [i] 滑动发音时,嘴型一定要从大到小滑动. [ɔi] 音与普通话拼音中的"凹"和前元音 [i] 音相似, 但不相同.普通话拼音中的"凹"音太放松, 而发合口双元音中的 [ɔ] 音时, 口型大圆放音, 后舌活动.发音结束时, 舌尖仍然抵下牙齿,不要闭嘴.

发音三要素	1. 唇势: 嘴型从大圆到很扁
	2. 齿距: 从两个半扁指滑动到半个扁指
	3. 舌位: 发音时, 从舌后部滑动到舌前部, 以唇势: 扁, 距: 半个扁指, 舌位: 舌尖紧抵下齿结束发音.

18. [iə] 开口双元音

开口双元音[iə]是由第一个元音 [i] 向第二个元音 [ə] 滑动发音时,嘴型一定要从小到大滑动.. [i] 音是元音字母 Ａａ 的尾音; [ə] 音与普通话中的 "阿" 音相似, 但不相同.从 [i] 音向 [ə] 音滑动发音时, 嘴型一定要从小到大滑动.发音结束时, 齿距仍然是两个扁指, 不要闭嘴.

发音三要素	1. 唇势: 扁　　2. 齿距: 从半个扁指滑动到两个扁指
	3. 舌位: 发音时,从舌前部滑动到舌中部,以唇势: 扁, 距: 两个扁指, 舌位: 舌中活动结束发[iə]音.

19. [εə] 开口双元音
开口双元音 [εə] 是由第一个元音 [ε] 向第二个元音 [ə] 滑动发音时，嘴型一定要从小到大滑动. [ε] 音的齿距是一个半扁指，是介于元音 [æ] (两个扁指) 和 [e] (一个扁指) 之间的音. [ə] 音与普通话中的"阿"音相似，但不相同.从 [ε] 音向 [ə] 音滑动发音时，嘴型一定要从小到大滑动.发音结束时，齿距仍然是两个扁指，不要闭嘴.

发音三要素	1. 唇势: 扁 2. 齿距: 从一个半扁指滑动到两个扁指 3. 舌位: 发音时，从舌前部滑动到舌中部，以唇势: 扁 齿距: 两个扁指 舌位: 舌中活动结束发 [εə] 音.

20. [uə] 开口双元音
开口双元音 [uə] 是由第一个元音 [u] 向第二个元音 [ə] 滑动发音时，嘴一定要从小到大滑动. [u] 音与普通话中的"屋"音相似，但不相同, [ə] 音与普通话中的"阿"音相似，也不相同. 从 [u] 音向 [ə] 音滑动发音时，嘴型一定要从小到大滑动. 发音结束时,齿距仍然是两个扁指,不要闭嘴.

发音三要素	1. 唇势: 从小圆到扁 2. 齿距: 从一个半扁指滑动到两个扁指 3. 舌位: 发音时,从舌后部滑动到舌中部,以唇势: 扁, 齿距: 两个扁指, 舌位: 舌中活动结束发 [uə] 音.

- 发音的三要素: 唇势 齿距 舌位

中国新移民学英语语音阶段要牢记的座右铭: 48 个国际音标与中文的发音，虽然有相似的音，但是没有一个是相同的音. 所以，发英语的每个音素都要按发音的三要素去检验.

英语辅音音素发音说明

1. [p] 双唇爆破音
[p] 和 [b] 是一对清,浊辅音. [p] 发音时, 双唇紧闭, 憋住一口气, 不能卷舌, 要平伸于口中, 不能碰到上齿和下齿, 然后让气流从口腔中突然冲开双唇的阻碍, 爆破成音. 发音时, 口腔部位与发 [b] 和 [m] 音的口腔部位相同. [p] 音与普通话中的"坡"的声母音相似, 但不相同, 需要去掉"坡"的声母音的尾音, 还要有爆破, 才能发出 [p] 音. 发音结束时, 口型是扁的, 张开的, 不要闭上嘴. 它是清辅音.
发音三要素　　1. 唇势: 双唇紧闭　　2. 齿距: 几乎闭合 　　　　　　　3. 舌位: 平伸于口中

2. [b] 双唇爆破音
[p] 和 [b] 是一对清,浊辅音. [b] 发音时, 双唇紧闭, 憋住一口气, 不能卷舌, 要平伸于口中, 不能碰到上齿和下齿, 然后让气流从口腔中突然冲开双唇的阻碍, 爆破成音. 发音时, 口腔部位与发 [p] 和 [m] 音的口腔部位相同. [b] 音与普通话中的"玻"的声母音相似, 但不相同, 需要去掉"玻"的声母音的尾音, 还要有爆破, 才能发出 [b] 音. 发音结束时, 口型是扁的, 张开的, 不要闭上嘴. 它是浊辅音.
发音三要素　　1. 唇势: 双唇紧闭　　2. 齿距: 几乎闭合 　　　　　　　3. 舌位: 平伸于口中

3. [t] 舌前 - 齿龈爆破音
[t] 和 [d] 是一对清,浊辅音. [t] 发音时,舌尖抵紧上齿龈, 憋住一口气, 形成阻力, 然后让气流从口腔中的舌尖和齿龈间突然冲出,爆破成音. 发音时,口腔部位与发 [d], [l] 和 [n] 音的口腔部位相同. [t] 音与普通话中"脱"的声母音相似, 但不相同. 需要去掉"脱"的声母音的尾音, 还要有爆破, 才能发出 [t] 音. 发音结束时,口型是扁的,张开的,不要闭上嘴. 它是清辅音.

发音三要素	1. 唇势: 扁　　　　　2. 齿距: 几乎闭合
	3. 舌位: 舌尖抵紧上齿龈

4. [d] 舌前 - 齿龈爆破音
[t] 和 [d] 是一对清,浊辅音. [d] 发音时, 舌尖抵紧上齿龈, 憋住一口气, 形成阻力, 然后让气流从口腔中的舌尖和齿龈间突然冲出, 爆破成音.发音时, 口腔部位与发 [t], [l] 和 [n] 音的口腔部位相同. [d] 音与普通话中的 "的" 的声母音相似, 但不相同. 得去掉 "的" 的声母音的尾音, 还要有爆破, 才能发出 [d] 音. 发音结束时, 口型是扁的, 张开的, 不要闭上嘴. 它是浊辅音.

发音三要素	1. 唇势: 扁　　　　　2. 齿距: 几乎闭合
	3. 舌位: 舌尖抵紧上齿龈

5. [k] 舌后 - 软颚爆破音
发音时, 舌跟贴近软颚, 憋住一口气, 形成阻力, 然后让气流从口腔中的舌跟和软颚间突然冲出, 爆破成音. 发音时, 口腔部位与发 [g] 和 [ŋ] 音的口腔部位相同. [k] 音与普通话中的 "科" 的声母音相似, 但不相同.要去掉 "科" 的声母音的尾音, 还要有爆破, 才能发出 [k] 音. 发音结束时, 口型是扁的, 张开的, 不要闭上嘴.它是清辅音. [k] 和 [g]是一对清,浊辅音.

发音三要素	1. 唇势: 扁　　　　　2. 齿距: 半个扁指
	3. 舌位: 舌跟贴近软颚

6. [g] 舌后 - 软颚爆破音
发音时,舌跟贴近软颚,憋住一口气,形成阻力,然后让气流从口腔中的舌跟和软颚间突然冲出, 爆破成音.发音时,口腔部位与发 [k] 和 [ŋ] 音的口腔部位相同. [g] 音与普通话中的 "哥" 的声母音相似, 但不相同. 要去掉 "哥" 的声母音的尾音, 还要有爆破, 才能发出 [g] 音.发音结束时, 口型是扁的, 张开的, 不要闭上嘴.它是浊辅音. [k] 和 [g] 是一对清,浊辅音.

发音三要素	1. 唇势: 扁　　　　　2. 齿距: 半个扁指
	3. 舌位: 舌跟贴近软颚

7. [f] 下唇 - 上齿摩擦音

[f]和[v]是一对清,浊辅音.[f]发音时,上齿咬住下唇,憋住一口气,形成阻力,然后让气流从上齿和下唇间冲出,摩擦成音.发音时,口腔部位与发[v]音的口腔部位相同.[f]音与普通话中的"夫"的声母音相似,但不相同.得去掉"夫"的声母音的尾音,还要让你的下唇和上齿摩擦,才能发出[f]音发音结束时,上齿仍然咬住下唇,不要松开.它是清辅音.

发音三要素	1. 唇势: 扁　　　　　2. 齿距: 下唇的厚度
	3. 舌位: 上齿咬住下唇, 舌平伸于口中

8. [v] 下唇 - 上齿摩擦音

[f]和[v]是一对清,浊辅音.[v]发音时,上齿咬住下唇,憋住一口气,形成阻力,然后让气流从上齿和下唇间冲出,摩擦成音.发音时,口腔部位与发[f]音的口腔部位相同.普通话中没有[v]音,可用上齿咬住下唇,憋住一口气,形成阻力,然后让气流从上齿和下唇间摩擦成"屋"音.发音结束时,上齿仍然咬住下唇,不要松开.它是浊辅音.

发音三要素	1. 唇势: 扁　　　　　2. 齿距: 下唇的厚度
	3. 舌位: 上齿咬住下唇, 舌平伸于口中

9. [s] 舌前 - 下齿摩擦音

[s]和[z]是一对清,浊辅音.[s]发音时,舌尖抵紧下齿,憋住一口气,形成阻力,然后让气流从舌尖和下齿间冲出,摩擦成音.发音时,口腔部位与发[z]音的口腔部位相同.[s]音与普通话拼音中的"s"音相似,但不相同.发音时,要用舌前和下齿摩擦发出[s]音.注意: 舌前和下齿摩擦发出[s]音比舌前和上齿摩擦发出[s]音更容易,更准确.发音结束时,舌尖仍然抵下齿,舌尖不要离开下齿.它是清辅音.

发音三要素	1. 唇势: 扁　　　　　2. 齿距: 闭合
	3. 舌位: 舌尖抵紧下齿

10. [z] 舌前－下齿摩擦音	
[s] 和 [z] 是一对清, 浊辅音. [z] 发音时, 舌尖抵紧下齿, 憋住一口气, 形成阻力, 然后让气流从舌尖和下齿间冲出, 摩擦成音. 发音时, 口腔部位与发 [s] 音的口腔部位相同. 普通话中没有 [z] 音, 可以用舌尖抵下齿, 憋住一口气, 形成阻力, 然后让气流从舌尖和下齿间摩擦成一个相似于普通话拼音中的 "r" 音. 但是, 这与普通话拼音中的 "r" 音不相同. 普通话拼音中的 "r" 音是卷舌音, 而国际音标 [z] 却不能卷舌 (国际音标中没有卷舌音. 发音时, 要用舌前和下齿摩擦才能发出 [z] 音. 发音要领是舌前和下齿摩擦发出 [s] 音. 比舌前和上齿摩擦发出 [s] 音更容易, 更准确. 发音结束时, 舌尖仍然抵下齿, 舌尖不要离开下齿. 它是浊辅音.	
发音三要素	1. 唇势: 扁　　　　2. 齿距: 闭合 3. 舌位: 舌尖抵紧下齿

11. [θ] 舌前－上齿外摩擦音	
[θ] 和 [ð] 是一对清, 浊辅音. [θ] 发音时, 舌前抵紧上齿外, 憋住一口气, 形成阻力, 然后让气流从舌前和上齿间冲出, 摩擦成音. 发音时, 口腔部位与发 [ð] 音的口腔部位相同. 普通话中没有 [θ] 音, 可以用舌前抵紧上齿外, 憋住一口气, 形成阻力, 然后用力让气流从舌前和上齿间摩擦成一个相似于普通话拼音中的 "s" 音. 与普通话拼音中的 "s" 音不相同之处在于, 要让舌前抵紧上齿外, 让气流从舌前和上齿间摩擦发出 [θ] 音. 发音结束时, 舌前仍然抵上齿外, 舌前不要离开上齿外. 它是清辅音.	
发音三要素	1. 唇势: 扁　　　　2. 齿距: 舌的厚度 3. 舌位: 舌前抵紧上齿外

12. [ð] 舌前－上齿外摩擦音	
[θ] 和 [ð] 是一对清, 浊辅音. [ð] 发音时, 舌前抵紧上齿外, 憋住一口气, 形成阻力, 然后让气流从舌前和上齿间冲出, 摩擦成音. 发音时, 口腔部位与发 [θ] 音的口腔部位相同. 普通话中没有 [ð] 音, 你可以用舌前抵紧上齿外, 憋住一口气, 形成阻力, 然后用力让气流从舌前和上齿间摩擦成	

一个相似于普通话拼音中的"r"音,但与普通话拼音中的"r"音不相同.普通话拼音中的"r"音是卷舌音,而国际音标 [ð] 却不能卷舌.发音时,要让舌前抵紧上齿外,让气流从舌前和上齿间摩擦才能发出 [ð]音.发音结束时,舌前仍然抵上齿外,舌前不要离开上齿外.它是浊辅音.

发音三要素	1. 唇势: 扁　　　　　　2. 齿距: 舌的厚度
	3. 舌位: 舌前抵紧上齿外

13. [ʃ] 舌中 - 硬颚摩擦音

[ʃ] 和 [ʒ] 是一对清, 浊辅音. [ʃ] 发音时, 舌中和硬颚靠近, 但要有间隙.此时, 憋住一口气, 形成阻力, 舌不能卷, 要平伸于口中, 不能碰到上齿和下齿, 然后让气流从舌中和硬颚间冲出, 摩擦成音.在发音时, 口腔部位与下面的 [ʒ] 的发音口腔部位相同.由于普通话中没有 [ʃ] 音, 需要让舌中和硬颚靠近, 但要有间隙.此时, 憋住一口气, 形成阻力, 然后用力让气流从舌中和硬颚间摩擦成一个相似于普通话拼音中的"sh"音.但与普通话拼音中"sh"音不相同.普通话拼音中"sh"音是卷舌音. 而 [ʃ] 却不能卷舌.要领是让舌中和硬颚靠近, 但要有间隙, 让气流从舌中和硬颚间摩擦才能发出 [ʃ] 音. 发音结束时, 舌中和硬颚间仍然有空隙, 保持发音时口型, 不要闭嘴.它是清辅音.

发音三要素	1. 唇势: 圆　　　　　　2. 齿距: 几乎闭合
	3. 舌位: 平伸于口中

\multicolumn{2}{c}{14. [ʒ] 舌中 - 硬颚摩擦音}
\multicolumn{2}{l}{[ʃ] 和 [ʒ] 是一对清, 浊辅音. [ʒ] 发音时, 舌中和硬颚靠近, 但有间隙, 此时, 憋住一口气, 形成阻力, 舌不能卷, 要平伸于口中, 不能碰到上齿和下齿, 然后让气流从舌中和硬颚间冲出, 摩擦成音.在发音时, 口腔部位与发 [ʃ] 音口腔部位相同.由于普通话中没有 [ʒ] 音, 需要让舌中和硬颚靠近, 但要有间隙.此时, 憋住一口气, 形成阻力, 然后用力让气流从舌中和硬颚间摩擦成一个相似于普通话拼音中的 "r" 音.但与普通话拼音中的 "r" 音不相同.普通话拼音中的 "r" 音是卷舌音, 而国际音标 [ʒ] 却不能卷舌.要领是让舌中和硬颚靠近, 但要有间隙, 让气流从舌中和硬颚间摩擦才能发出 [ʒ] 音.发音结束时, 舌中和硬颚间仍然有空隙, 保持发音时的口型, 不要闭嘴.它是浊辅音.}
发音三要素	1. 唇势: 圆 2. 齿距: 几乎闭合 3. 舌位: 平伸于口中

\multicolumn{2}{c}{15. [h] 声门摩擦音}
\multicolumn{2}{l}{发音时,用声门挡住气流,此时, 憋住一口气,形成阻力, 不能卷舌,要平伸于口中,不能碰到上齿和下齿,然后让气流从声门冲出,摩擦成音. [h] 音与普通话中的 "喝" 的声母音相似,但不相同.要去掉 "喝" 的声母音的尾音,还要让气流从声门冲出,摩擦成 [h] 音.发音结束时,可以松口气,但是要保持发音时的口型,不要闭嘴.它是清辅音.}
发音三要素	1. 唇势: 扁 2. 齿距: 一个扁指 3. 舌位: 平伸于口中

\multicolumn{2}{c}{16. [j] 舌前 - 硬颚摩擦音}
\multicolumn{2}{l}{发音时,舌前和硬颚间有空隙,此时,憋住一口气,形成阻力, 舌尖抵下齿.嘴唇是扁的,上下牙齿几乎闭合,然后让气流从舌前和硬颚间冲出, 摩擦成音. [j] 音与普通话中 "耶" 的声母音相似,但不相同.要去掉 "耶" 的声母音的尾音,还要让气流从舌前和硬颚间冲出,摩擦成 [j] 音.发音结束时,可松口气,但要保持发音时的口型,不要闭嘴.它是浊辅音.}

发音三要素	1. 唇势: 扁　　　　　　2. 齿距: 几乎闭合
	3. 舌位: 舌尖抵下齿

17. [w] 舌后-软颚摩擦音

发音时,舌后和软颚间要有空隙,此时,憋住一口气,形成阻力,不能卷舌,要平伸于口中,不能碰到上齿和下齿,然后让气流从舌后和软颚间冲出,摩擦成音.[w]音与普通话中的"窝"的声母音相似,但不相同.要去掉"窝"的声母音的尾音,还要让气流从舌后和软颚间冲出,摩擦成[w]音.发音结束时,可以松口气,但是要保持发音时的口型,不要闭嘴.它是浊辅音.

发音三要素	1. 唇势: 圆　　　　　　2. 齿距: 几乎闭合
	3. 舌位: 平伸于口中

18. [r] 舌中 - 硬颚摩擦音

发音时, 舌中和硬颚间要有空隙, 此时, 憋住一口气, 形成阻力, 不能卷舌, 要平伸于口中, 不要碰到上齿和下齿, 然后让气流从舌中和硬颚间冲出, 摩擦成音. [r] 音与普通话中的"若"的声母音相似, 但不相同. "若"是卷舌音, 是四声, 而国际音标 [r] 却不能卷舌, [r] 是一声. 发音结束时, 可以松口气, 但是要保持发音时的口型, 舌仍然平伸于口中, 不要闭嘴.它是浊辅音.

发音三要素	1. 唇势: 圆　　　　　　2. 齿距: 几乎闭合
	3. 舌位: 平伸于口中

19. [l] 舌前 - 齿龈舌侧音或旁流音

辅音字母 l 在单词中发 [l] 音.发音时, 舌尖抵紧上齿龈, 憋住一口气, 形成阻力, 然后让气流从口腔中的舌尖和齿龈两旁突然冲出, 摩擦成 [l] 音.发音时, 口腔部位与发 [t], [d] 和 [n] 音的口腔部位相同. [l] 音与普通话中"欧"相似, 但不相同.发音结束时, 可以松口气, 但是要保持发音时的口型, 舌尖离开上齿龈, 不要闭嘴.它是浊辅音.

发音三要素	1. 唇势: 扁　　　　　　2. 齿距: 几乎闭合
	3. 舌位: 舌尖抵紧上齿龈

1 [l]
辅音字母 l 在词首或元音前发 [l] 音.发音时,舌尖抵紧上齿龈,憋住一口气,形成阻力,然后让气流从口腔中的舌尖和齿龈两旁突然冲出,摩擦成音.音从舌两旁流出音时,舌尖离开上齿龈.发音时,口腔部位与发 [t],[d] 和 [n] 音的口腔部位相同. [l] 音与普通话中的"了"的声母音相似,但不相同.要去掉"了"的声母音的尾音,还要让气流从口腔中的舌尖和齿龈两旁突然冲出,摩擦成 [l] 音去拼后面的元音.发音结束时,可以松口气,但是要保持发音时的口型,舌尖离开上齿龈,不要闭嘴.它是浊辅音.

发音三要素	1. 唇势: 扁　　　　2. 齿距: 几乎闭合 3. 舌位: 舌尖抵紧上齿龈,音从舌两旁流出音后,舌尖离开上齿龈

20. [m] 双唇-鼻音
辅音字母 m 在单词中发 [m] 音.发音时,双唇紧闭,憋住一口气,不能卷舌,要平伸于口中,不能碰到上齿和下齿,也不能让气流从口腔中出来,要让气流从鼻腔发出 [m] 音.发音时,口腔部位与发 [p] 和 [b] 音的口腔部位相同. [m] 音与普通话中的"牡"的声母音的一声音相似,而"牡"音在普通话中是三声音,但与"牡"的声母音不相同.要去掉"牡"的声母音的尾音,还要双唇紧闭,憋住一口气,让气流从鼻腔发出 [m] 音.发音结束时,可以松口气,但是要保持发音时的口型,不要张开口.它是浊辅音.

发音三要素	1. 唇势: 双唇紧闭　　　2. 齿距: 几乎闭合 3. 舌位: 平伸于口中

m [m]
辅音字母 m 在词首或元音前发 [m] 音发音时,双唇紧闭,憋住一口气,不能卷舌,要平伸于口中,不能碰到上齿和下齿,也不能让气流从口腔中出来.要让气流从鼻腔发出 [m] 音. 发音时,口腔部位与发 [p] 和

[b] 音的口腔部位相同. [m] 在拼它后边的元音时,它的音与普通话拼音中的 "m" 音相似, 但要去掉 "m" 音的尾音, 还要双唇紧闭, 憋住一口气, 让气流从鼻腔发出 [m] 音来拼它后面的元音. 它是浊辅音.

发音三要素	1. 唇势: 双唇紧闭 2. 齿距: 几乎闭合 3. 舌位: 平伸于口中

21. [n] 舌前-齿龈鼻音

辅音字母 n 在单词中发 [n] 音. 发音时, 舌尖抵紧上齿龈, 憋住一口气, 形成阻力, 不能让气流从口腔中出来, 要让气流从鼻腔中发出 [n] 音. 发音时, 口腔部位与发 [t], [d] 和 [l] 音的口腔部位相同. [n] 音与普通话中的 "呢" 的声母音相似, 但不相同, 要去掉 "呢" 的声母音的尾音, 还要舌尖抵紧上齿龈, 憋住一口气, 形成阻力, 让气流从鼻腔中发出 [n] 音. 发音结束时, 可以松口气, 但是要保持发音时的口型, 不要闭嘴. 舌尖不要离开上齿龈. 它是浊辅音.

发音三要素	1. 唇势: 扁 2. 齿距: 几乎闭合 3. 舌位: 舌尖抵紧上齿龈

n [n]

辅音字母 n 在词首或元音前发 [n] 音. 发音时, 舌尖抵紧上齿龈, 憋住一口气, 形成阻力, 不能让气流从口腔中出来, 要让气流从鼻腔中发出 [n] 音. 发音时, 口腔部位与发 [t], [d] 和 [l] 音的口腔部位相同. [n] 在拼它后边的元音时, 它的音与普通话拼音中的 "n" 音相似, 但要去掉 "n" 音的尾音, 还要舌尖抵紧上齿龈, 憋住一口气, 形成阻力, 让气流从鼻腔中发出 [n] 音来拼它后边的元音. 它是浊辅音.

	1. 唇势: 扁 2. 齿距: 几乎闭合 3. 舌位: 舌尖抵紧上齿龈

22. [ŋ] 舌后-软腭鼻音

发音时,舌跟贴近软腭,憋住一口气,形成阻力,不能让气流从口腔中出来,要让气流从鼻腔中发出 [ŋ] 音.发音时,口腔部位与发 [k] 和 [g] 音的口腔部位相同. [ŋ] 音与普通话拼音中的 "ing" 音的尾音相似,但不相同.得让你的舌跟贴近软腭,憋住一口气,形成阻力,让气流从鼻腔中发出 [ŋ] 音.发音结束时,可以松口气,但是要保持发音时的口型,不要闭嘴.舌跟和软腭间仍然有空隙.它是浊辅音.

发音三要素	1. 唇势: 扁　　　　　　2. 齿距: 半个扁指
	3. 舌位: 舌跟贴近软腭

23. [tr] 破擦音 (既有爆破音又有摩擦音)

[tr] 和 [dr] 是一对清,浊辅音.发 [tr] 音时,舌尖抵紧上齿龈,憋住一口气,形成阻力,然后发 [t] 音,但不要发出 [t] 音,就发 [r] 音,使之摩擦成 [tr] 音.发音时,口腔部位与发 [dr] 音的口腔部位相同. [tr] 音与普通话中的 "戳" 音相似,但不相同.普通话中的 "戳" 是卷舌音,而 [tr] 却不能有卷舌音.要领是破擦音[tr]中的[t]音要不完全爆破,而[r]音却要摩擦.发音结束时,可以松口气,但是舌仍然平伸于口中,不要闭嘴.它是清辅音.

发音三要素	1. 唇势: 圆　　　　　　2. 齿距: 几乎闭合
	3. 舌位: 首先舌尖抵紧上齿龈,然后舌中和硬腭间有空隙.

24. [dr] 破擦音 (既有爆破音又有摩擦音)

[tr] 和 [dr] 是一对清,浊辅音. [dr] 发音时,舌尖抵紧上齿龈,憋住一口气,形成阻力,然后发 [d] 音,但不要发出 [d] 音,就发 [r] 音,使之摩擦成 [dr] 音.发音时,口腔部位与发 [tr] 音的口腔部位相同. [dr] 音与普通话中的 "桌" 音相似,但不相同.普通话中的 "桌" 是卷舌音,而 [dr] 却不能有卷舌音.要领是破擦音 [dr] 中的 [d] 音要不完全爆破,而 [r] 音却要摩擦.发音结束时,可以松口气,但是舌仍然平伸

	于口中,不要闭嘴.它是浊辅音.
发音三要素	1. 唇势: 圆　　　　　　2. 齿距: 几乎闭合 3. 舌位: 首先舌尖抵紧上齿龈,然后舌中和硬颚间有空隙.

25. [ts] 破擦音 (既有爆破音又有摩擦音)	
[ts] 和 [dz] 是一对清,浊辅音. [ts] 发音时,舌尖抵紧上齿龈,憋住一口气,形成阻力,然后让你的舌头顺着上齿龈一直刮止下牙齿摩擦成 [ts] 音.发音时,口腔部位与发 [dz] 音的口腔部位相同. [ts] 音与普通话拼音中的"c"音相似,但不相同.要领是破擦音 [ts] 中的[t]音要不完全爆破,而 [s] 音却要摩擦.发音结束时,舌尖仍然抵下齿,舌尖不要离开下齿.它是清辅音.	
发音三要素	1. 唇势: 扁　　　　　　2. 齿距: 几乎闭合 3. 舌位: 舌尖抵紧上齿龈,然后舌头顺着上齿龈一直止下牙齿摩擦成音

26. [dz] 破擦音 (既有爆破音又有摩擦音)	
[ts] 和 [dz] 是一对清,浊辅音. [dz] 发音时,舌尖抵紧上齿龈,憋住一口气,形成阻力,然后用舌头顺着上齿龈一直刮止下牙齿摩擦成 [dz] 音.发音时,口腔部位与发 [ts] 音的口腔部位相同. [dz] 音与普通话拼音中的"z"音相似,但不相同.要领是破擦音 [dz] 中的 [d] 音要不完全爆破,而 [z] 音却要摩擦.发音结束时,舌尖仍然抵下齿,舌尖不要离开下齿.它是浊辅音.	
发音三要素	1. 唇势: 扁　　　　　　2. 齿距: 几乎闭合 3. 舌位: 舌尖抵紧上齿龈,然后舌头顺着上齿龈一直止下牙齿摩擦成音

27. [tʃ] 破擦音（既有爆破音又有摩擦音）

[tʃ] 和 [dʒ] 是一对清, 浊辅音. [tʃ] 发音时, 舌尖抵紧上齿龈, 憋住一口气, 形成阻力, 然后发 [t] 音, 但不要发出 [t] 音, 就发 [ʃ] 音, 使之摩擦成 [tʃ] 音. 发音时, 口腔部位与发 [dʒ] 音的口腔部位相同. [tʃ] 音与普通话拼音中的 "ch" 音相似, 但不相同. 普通话拼音中的 "ch" 是卷舌音, 而 [tʃ] 却不能有卷舌音. 要领是破擦音 [tʃ] 中的[t]音要不完全爆破, 而[ʃ]音却要摩擦. 发音结束时, 可以松口气, 但是舌仍然要平伸于口中, 不要闭嘴. 它是清辅音.

发音三要素	1. 唇势: 圆　　　　　　2. 齿距: 几乎闭合 3. 舌位: 首先舌尖抵紧上齿龈, 然后舌中和硬颚间要空隙

28. [dʒ] 破擦音（既有爆破音又有摩擦音）

[tʃ] 和 [dʒ] 是一对清, 浊辅音. [dʒ] 发音时, 舌尖抵紧上齿龈, 憋住一口气, 形成阻力, 然后发 [d] 音, 但不要发出 [d] 音, 就发 [ʒ] 音, 使之摩擦成 [dʒ] 音. 发音时, 口腔部位与发 [tʃ] 音的口腔部位相同. [dʒ] 音与普通话拼音中的 "zh" 音相似, 但不相同. 普通话拼音中的 "zh" 是卷舌音, 而 [dʒ] 却不能有卷舌音. 要领是破擦音 [dʒ]中的 [d] 音要不完全爆破, 而 [ʒ] 音却要摩擦. 发音结束时, 可以松口气, 但是舌仍然要平伸于口中, 不要闭嘴. 它是浊辅音.

发音三要素	1. 唇势: 圆　　　　　　2. 齿距: 几乎闭合 3. 舌位: 首先舌尖抵紧上齿龈, 然后舌中和硬颚间要空隙

发音的三要素: 唇势 齿距 舌位

中国新移民学英语语音阶段要牢记的座右铭: 48 个国际音标与中文的发音, 虽然有相似的音, 但是没有一个是相同的音. 所以, 发英语的每个音素都要按发音的三要素去检验.

Linan Shi & Shasha Shi

英 语 音 素 发 音 说 明

1. [i:] 前元音	
前元音, 即舌前部（舌尖）活动. [i:] 音与普通话中的"一"音相似, 但不相同. 发 [i:] 音时, 音要发得长点, 因为有长音符号. [i:] 是长元音. 发音结束时, 舌尖仍然抵住下牙齿.	
发音三要素	1. 唇势: 最扁 2. 齿距: 几乎闭合 3. 舌位: 舌尖抵紧下牙齿

2. [i] 前元音	
前元音,即舌前部(舌尖) 活动. [i] 音是元音字母 A a 的尾音. 不要发成普通话中的"一"音, 因为"一"音太长, 而 [i] 音是短元音. [i] 音是 [ei] 音的尾音, 并不是 [i:] 音的短音. 发音结束时,舌尖仍然抵住下牙齿.	
发音三要素	1. 唇势: 扁 2. 齿距: 半个扁指 3. 舌位: 舌尖抵紧下牙齿

3. [e] 前元音	
前元音, 即舌前部 (舌尖) 活动. [e] 音与普通话中的"艾"音相似,但不相同. 普通话中的"艾"音太长, 而前元音 [e] 音是短元音. 发音结束时, 舌尖仍然抵住下牙齿.	
发音三要素	1. 唇势: 扁 2. 齿距: 一个扁指 3. 舌位: 舌尖抵紧下牙齿

4. [æ] 前元音	
前元音, 即舌前部活动. 舌前部就是舌尖. [æ] 音与普通话中的"碍"音相似, 但不相同. 普通话中的"碍"音太长, 而前元音 [æ] 音是短元音. 在发音结束时, 舌尖仍然抵住下牙齿.	
发音三要素	1. 唇势: 扁 2. 齿距: 两个扁指 3. 舌位: 舌尖抵紧下牙齿

5. [ʌ] 中元音	
中元音, 即舌中部（舌端）活动. [ʌ] 音与普通话中的"呵"音相似, 但不相同. 普通话中的"呵"音太长, 开口太大, 而中元音 [ʌ] 音是短元音. 发音结束时, 仍然保持原来的口型, 不要闭嘴.	
发音三要素	1. 唇势: 扁 2. 齿距: 两个扁指 3. 舌位: 舌头平伸于口中, 舌前部不要碰到上齿和下齿, 舌中部在发音时抬高

6. [ə] 中元音	
中元音, 即舌中部（舌端）活动. [ə] 音与普通话中的"阿"音相似, 但不相同. 普通话中的"阿"音太长, 开口太大, 而中元音 [ə] 音是短元音. 发音结束时, 仍然保持原来的口型, 不要闭嘴.	
发音三要素	1. 唇势: 扁　　　　　2. 齿距: 两个扁指 3. 舌位: 舌头平伸于口中, 舌前部不要碰到上齿和下齿, 舌中部在发音时抬高

7. [ə:] 中元音	
中元音, 即舌中部（舌端）活动. [ə:] 音与普通话中"饿"音相似, 但不相同. 普通话中的"饿"音太放松, 而发中元音 [ə:] 音时, 口腔稍紧张. [ə:] 是长元音, 发音结束时, 仍然保持原来的口型, 不要闭嘴.	
发音三要素	1. 唇势: 扁　　　　　2. 齿距: 两个扁指 3. 舌位: 舌头平伸于口中, 舌前部不要碰到上齿和下齿, 舌中部在发音时抬高.

8. [ɑ:] 后元音	
后元音, 即舌后部(舌根)活动. [ɑ:] 音与普通话中的"啊"音相似, 但不相同. 普通话中的"啊"音太放松, 而发后元音 [ɑ:] 音时, 口全开, 舌头平伸于口中. 舌前部和舌中部都不要碰到上齿和下齿, 舌后部要下压. [ɑ:] 是长元音, 发音结束时, 仍然保持原来的口型, 不要闭嘴.	

发音三要素	1. 唇势: 口全开椭圆形　　2. 齿距: 三个扁指
	3. 舌位: 舌头平伸于口中,舌前部和舌中部都不要碰到上齿和下齿,发音时舌后部下压.

9. [ɔ] 后元音

后元音,即舌后部(舌根)活动. [ɔ] 音与普通话中的"凹"音相似,但不相同. 普通话中的"凹"音太放松,而发后元音 [ɔ] 音时,口是大圆形,舌头平伸于口中,舌前部和舌中部都不要碰到上齿和下齿,舌后部要下压,尽量要向外放音. [ɔ] 是短元音. 发音结束时,仍然保持原来的口型,不要闭嘴.

发音三要素	1. 唇势: 大圆形　　2. 齿距: 两个半扁指
	3. 舌位: 舌头平伸于口中,舌前部和舌中部都不要碰到上齿和下齿,发音时舌后部下压.

10. [ɔː] 后元音

后元音,即舌后部(舌根)活动. [ɔː] 音与普通话中的"奥"音相似,但不相同.普通话中的"奥"音太放松,而发后元音 [ɔː] 音时,口是大圆形,舌头平伸于口中,舌前部和舌中部都不要碰到上齿和下齿,舌后部要下压,尽量要向外放音. [ɔː] 是长元音. 发音结束时,仍然保持原来的口型,不要闭嘴.

发音三要素	1. 唇势: 大圆形　　2. 齿距: 两个半扁指
	3. 舌位: 舌头平伸于口中,舌前部和舌中部都不要碰到上齿和下齿,发音时舌后部下压

11. [u] 后元音

后元音,即舌后部（舌根）活动. [u] 音与普通话中的"屋"音相似,但不相同.普通话中的"屋"音太放松,而发后元音 [u] 音时,口是小圆形,舌头平伸于口中,舌前部和舌中部都不要碰到上齿和下齿.发音时, 舌后部要上抬,尽量要向里拢音. [u] 是短元音, 发音结束时, 仍然保持原来的口型, 不要闭嘴.

发音三要素	1. 唇势: 小圆形　　2. 齿距: 一个半扁指 3. 舌位: 舌头平伸于口中, 舌前部和舌中部都不要碰到上齿和下齿, 发音时舌后部上抬

12. [u:] 后元音	
后元音, 即舌后部（舌根）活动. [u:] 音与普通话中的"务"音相似, 但不相同. 普通话中的"务"音太放松, 而发后元音 [u:] 音时, 口是小圆形. 舌头平伸于口中, 舌前部和舌中部都不要碰到上齿和下齿. 发音时, 舌后部要上抬, 尽量要向里拢音. [u:] 是长元音. 发音结束时, 仍然保持原来的口型, 不要闭嘴.	
发音三要素	1. 唇势: 口是小圆形　　2. 齿距: 一个半扁指 3. 舌位: 舌头平伸于口中. 舌前部和舌中部都不要碰到上齿和下齿, 发音时舌后部上抬

13. [e i] 合口双元音	
合口双元音 [e i] 是由第一个元音 [e] 向第二个元音 [i] 滑动发音时, 嘴型一定要从大到小滑动. [e i] 音与普通话拼音中的 "e i" 音相似, 但不相同. 普通话拼音中的 "ei" 音太放松, 嘴型大, 且没有滑动. 而发合口双元音 [e i] 音时, 由第一个元音 [e] 向第二个元音 [i] 滑动, 嘴型一定要从大到小滑动, 才能发出合口双元音 [e i] 音. 发音结束时, 舌尖仍然抵下牙齿, 不要闭嘴.	
发音三要素	1. 唇势: 扁　　2. 齿距: 从一个扁指滑动到半个扁指 3. 舌位: 舌前部紧抵下齿

14. [a i] 合口双元音	
合口双元音 [a i] 是由第一个元音 [a] 向第二个元音 [i] 滑动发音时, 嘴型一定要从大到小滑动. [a i] 音与普通话拼音中的 "啊" 和合口双元音 [e i] 的第二个元音 [i] 的发音相似, 但不相同. 普通话拼音中的 "啊" 音太放松, 而发合口双元音中的 [a] 音时, 口全开, 舌下压. 因此, 发合口双元音 [a i] 音时, 要由第一个元音 [a] 向第二个元音 [i]	

滑动，嘴型一定要从大到小滑动，才能发出合口双元音［ａｉ］音. 发音结束时，舌尖仍然抵下牙齿，不要闭嘴.

发音三要素	1. 唇势: 嘴型从口全开滑动到很扁 2. 齿距: 从三个扁指滑动到半个扁指 3. 舌位: 从舌后部活动滑动到舌前部，发音后，以舌尖紧抵下牙齿结束发音

15.［ａｕ］合口双元音

合口双元音［ａｕ］是由第一个元音［ａ］向第二个元音［ｕ］滑动发音时，嘴型一定要从大到小滑动.［ａｕ］音与普通话拼音中的"啊"和后元音［ｕ］音相似，但不相同.普通话拼音中的"啊"音太放松，而合口双元音中的［ａ］音时，口全开，舌下压. 发音结束时，嘴型是小圆.

发音三要素	1. 唇势: 嘴型从口全开滑动到小圆 2. 齿距: 从三个扁指滑动到一个半个扁指 3. 舌位: 发音时，舌后部从下压放音滑动到舌后部上拢音.以唇势: 小圆，齿距: 一个半扁指，舌位: 后部上抬拢音结束发音

16.［əｕ］合口双元音

合口双元音［əｕ］是由第一个元音［ə］向第二个元音［ｕ］滑动发音时，嘴型一定要从大到小滑动.［əｕ］音与普通话拼音中的"沤"音相似，但不相同. 普通话拼音中的"沤"音只有一个音，而发合口双元音［əｕ］音时，要由第一个元音［ə］向第二个元音［ｕ］音滑动，嘴型一定要从大到小滑动，才能发出合口双元音［əｕ］音. 发音结束时，嘴型是小圆.

发音三要素	1. 唇势: 嘴型从扁到小圆 2. 齿距: 从两个扁指滑动到一个半个扁指 3. 舌位: 发音时，从舌中部滑动到舌后部上抬拢音. 以唇势: 小圆，齿距: 一个半个扁指，舌位: 舌后部上抬拢音结束发音

17. [ɔi] 合口双元音	
合口双元音 [ɔi] 是由第一个元音 [ɔ] 向第二个元音 [i] 滑动发音时,嘴型一定要从大到小滑动. [ɔi] 音与普通话拼音中的"凹"和前元音 [i] 音相似,但不相同.普通话拼音中的"凹"音太放松,而发合口双元音中的 [ɔ] 音时,口型大圆放音,后舌活动.发音结束时,舌尖仍然抵下牙齿,不要闭嘴.	
发音三要素	1. 唇势: 嘴型从大圆到很扁 2. 齿距: 从两个半扁指滑动到半个扁指 3. 舌位: 发音时,从舌后部滑动到舌前部,以唇势: 扁,距: 半个扁指, 舌位: 舌尖紧抵下齿结束发音.

18. [iə] 开口双元音	
开口双元音[iə]是由第一个元音 [i] 向第二个元音 [ə] 滑动发音时,嘴型一定要从小到大滑动.. [i] 音是元音字母 A a 的尾音; [ə] 音与普通话中的"阿"音相似,但不相同.从 [i] 音向 [ə] 音滑动发音时,嘴型一定要从小到大滑动.发音结束时, 齿距仍然是两个扁指, 不要闭嘴.	
发音三要素	1. 唇势: 扁 2. 齿距: 从半个扁指滑动到两个扁指 3. 舌位: 发音时,从舌前部滑动到舌中部,以唇势: 扁,距: 两个扁指, 舌位: 舌中活动结束发 [iə] 音.

19. [ɛə] 开口双元音	
开口双元音 [ɛə] 是由第一个元音 [ɛ] 向第二个元音 [ə] 滑动发音时, 嘴型一定要从小到大滑动. [ɛ] 音的齿距是一个半扁指, 是介于元音 [æ] (两个扁指) 和 [e] (一个扁指) 之间的音. [ə] 音与普通话中的"阿"音相似, 但不相同.从 [ɛ] 音向[ə]音滑动发音时, 嘴型一定要从小到大滑动.发音结束时, 齿距仍然是两个扁指, 不要闭嘴.	
发音三要素	1. 唇势: 扁 2. 齿距: 从一个半扁指滑动到两个扁指 3. 舌位: 发音时,从舌前部滑动到舌中部,以唇势: 扁 齿距: 两个扁指 舌位: 舌中活动结束发 [ɛə] 音.

20. [uə] 开口双元音	
开口双元音 [uə] 是由第一个元音 [u] 向第二个元音 [ə] 滑动发音时, 嘴一定要从小到大滑动. [u] 音与普通话中的"屋"音相似, 但不相同, [ə] 音与普通话中的"阿"音相似, 也不相同. 从 [u] 音向 [ə] 音滑动发音时, 嘴型一定要从小到大滑动. 发音结束时,齿距仍然是两个扁指,不要闭嘴.	
发音三要素	1. 唇势: 从小圆到扁 2. 齿距: 从一个半扁指滑动到两个扁指 3. 舌位: 发音时,从舌后部滑动到舌中部,以唇势: 扁, 齿距: 两个扁指, 舌位: 舌中活动结束发 [uə] 音.

21. [p] 双唇爆破音	
[p] 和 [b] 是一对清,浊辅音. [p] 发音时,双唇紧闭,憋住一口气,不能卷舌, 要平伸于口中, 不能碰到上齿和下齿, 然后让气流从口腔中突然冲开双唇的阻碍, 爆破成音. 发音时, 口腔部位与发 [b] 和 [m] 音的口腔部位相同. [p] 音与普通话中的"坡"的声母音相似, 但不相同, 需要去掉"坡"的声母音的尾音, 还要有爆破, 才能发出 [p] 音. 发音结束时, 口型是扁的, 张开的, 不要闭上嘴. 它是清辅音.	
发音三要素	1. 唇势: 双唇紧闭　　　2. 齿距: 几乎闭合 3. 舌位: 平伸于口中

22. [b] 双唇爆破音	
[p] 和 [b] 是一对清,浊辅音. [b] 发音时, 双唇紧闭, 憋住一口气, 不能卷舌, 要平伸于口中, 不能碰到上齿和下齿, 然后让气流从口腔中突然冲开双唇的阻碍, 爆破成音. 发音时,口腔部位与发 [p] 和 [m] 音的口腔部位相同. [b] 音与普通话中的"玻"的声母音相似, 但不相同, 需要去掉"玻"的声母音的尾音, 还要有爆破, 才能发出 [b] 音. 发音结束时, 口型是扁的, 张开的, 不要闭上嘴. 它是浊辅音.	
发音三要素	1. 唇势: 双唇紧闭　　　2. 齿距: 几乎闭合 3. 舌位: 平伸于口中

23. [t] 舌前 - 齿龈爆破音	
[t] 和 [d] 是一对清,浊辅音. [t] 发音时,舌尖抵紧上齿龈,憋住一口气,形成阻力,然后让气流从口腔中的舌尖和齿龈间突然冲出,爆破成音.发音时,口腔部位与发[d], [l] 和 [n] 音的口腔部位相同. [t] 音与普通话中"脱"的声母音相似,但不相同.需要去掉"脱"的声母音的尾音,还要有爆破,才能发出 [t] 音.发音结束时,口型是扁的,张开的,不要闭上嘴.它是清辅音.	
发音三要素	1. 唇势: 扁　　　　2. 齿距: 几乎闭合 3. 舌位: 舌尖抵紧上齿龈

24. [d] 舌前 - 齿龈爆破音	
[t] 和 [d] 是一对清,浊辅音. [d] 发音时,舌尖抵紧上齿龈,憋住一口气,形成阻力,然后让气流从口腔中的舌尖和齿龈间突然冲出,爆破成音.发音时,口腔部位与发 [t], [l] 和 [n] 音的口腔部位相同. [d] 音与普通话中的"的"的声母音相似,但不相同. 得去掉"的"的声母音的尾音,还要有爆破,才能发出 [d] 音. 发音结束时,口型是扁的,张开的,不要闭上嘴. 它是浊辅音.	
发音三要素	1. 唇势: 扁　　　　2. 齿距: 几乎闭合 3. 舌位: 舌尖抵紧上齿龈

25. [k] 舌后 - 软颚爆破音	
发音时, 舌跟贴近软颚, 憋住一口气, 形成阻力, 然后让气流从口腔中的舌跟和软颚间突然冲出, 爆破成音. 发音时, 口腔部位与发 [g] 和 [ŋ] 音的口腔部位相同. [k] 音与普通话中的 "科" 的声母音相似, 但不相同.要去掉 "科" 的声母音的尾音, 还要有爆破, 才能发出 [k] 音. 发音结束时, 口型是扁的, 张开的, 不要闭上嘴.它是清辅音. [k] 和 [g] 是一对清,浊辅音.	
发音三要素	1. 唇势: 扁　　　　2. 齿距: 半个扁指 3. 舌位: 舌跟贴近软颚

26. [g] 舌后 - 软颚爆破音	
发音时,舌跟贴近软颚,憋住一口气,形成阻力,然后让气流从口腔中的舌跟和软颚间突然冲出,爆破成音.发音时,口腔部位与发 [k] 和 [ŋ] 音的口腔部位相同. [g] 音与普通话中的"哥"的声母音相似,但不相同. 要去掉"哥"的声母音的尾音, 还要有爆破, 才能发出 [g] 音.发音结束时, 口型是扁的, 张开的, 不要闭上嘴.它是浊辅音. [k] 和 [g] 是一对清,浊辅音.	
发音三要素	1. 唇势: 扁　　　　　　2. 齿距: 半个扁指 3. 舌位: 舌跟贴近软颚

27. [f] 下唇 - 上齿摩擦音	
[f] 和 [v] 是一对清, 浊辅音. [f] 发音时, 上齿咬住下唇, 憋住一口气,形成阻力, 然后让气流从上齿和下唇间冲出, 摩擦成音.发音时, 口腔部位与发 [v] 音的口腔部位相同. [f] 音与普通话中的"夫"的声母音相似, 但不相同.得去掉"夫"的声母音的尾音, 还要让你的下唇和上齿摩擦, 才能发出 [f] 音发音结束时, 上齿仍然咬住下唇,不要松开.它是清辅音.	
发音三要素	1. 唇势: 扁　　　　　　2. 齿距: 下唇的厚度 3. 舌位: 上齿咬住下唇, 舌平伸于口中

28. [v] 下唇 - 上齿摩擦音	
[f] 和 [v] 是一对清, 浊辅音. [v] 发音时, 上齿咬住下唇, 憋住一口气, 形成阻力, 然后让气流从上齿和下唇间冲出, 摩擦成音.发音时, 口腔部位与发 [f] 音的口腔部位相同.普通话中没有 [v] 音, 可用上齿咬住下唇, 憋住一口气, 形成阻力, 然后让气流从上齿和下唇间摩擦成"屋"音.发音结束时, 上齿仍然咬住下唇, 不要松开.它是浊辅音.	
发音三要素	1. 唇势: 扁　　　　　　2. 齿距: 下唇的厚度 3. 舌位: 上齿咬住下唇, 舌平伸于口中

	29. [s] 舌前 - 下齿摩擦音
	[s] 和 [z] 是一对清, 浊辅音. [s] 发音时, 舌尖抵紧下齿, 憋住一口气, 形成阻力, 然后让气流从舌尖和下齿间冲出, 摩擦成音.发音时, 口腔部位与发 [z] 音的口腔部位相同. [s] 音与普通话拼音中的 "s" 音相似, 但不相同.发音时, 要用舌前和下齿摩擦发出 [s] 音.注意: 舌前和下齿摩擦发出 [s] 音比舌前和上齿摩擦发出 [s] 音更容易, 更准确. 发音结束时, 舌尖仍然抵下齿, 舌尖不要离开下齿.它是清辅音.
发音三要素	1. 唇势: 扁　　　　　2. 齿距: 闭合 3. 舌位: 舌尖抵紧下齿

	30. [z] 舌前 - 下齿摩擦音
	[s] 和 [z] 是一对清, 浊辅音. [z] 发音时, 舌尖抵紧下齿, 憋住一口气, 形成阻力, 然后让气流从舌尖和下齿间冲出, 摩擦成音.发音时, 口腔部位与发 [s] 音的口腔部位相同.普通话中没有 [z] 音, 可以用舌尖抵下齿, 憋住一口气, 形成阻力, 然后让气流从舌尖和下齿间摩擦成一个相似于普通话拼音中的 "r" 音. 但是, 这与普通话拼音中的 "r" 音不相同. 普通话拼音中的 "r" 音是卷舌音, 而国际音标 [z] 却不能卷舌 (国际音标中没有卷舌音.发音时, 要用舌前和下齿摩擦才能发出 [z] 音.发音要领是舌前和下齿摩擦发出 [s] 音.比舌前和上齿摩擦发出 [s] 音更容易, 更准确.发音结束时, 舌尖仍然抵下齿, 舌尖不要离开下齿. 它是浊辅音.
发音三要素	1. 唇势: 扁　　　　　2. 齿距: 闭合 3. 舌位: 舌尖抵紧下齿

	31. [θ] 舌前 - 上齿外摩擦音
	[θ] 和 [ð] 是一对清, 浊辅音. [θ] 发音时,舌前抵紧上齿外,憋住一口气, 形成阻力,然后让气流从舌前和上齿间冲出,摩擦成音.发音时, 口腔部位与发 [ð] 音的口腔部位相同.普通话中没有 [θ] 音, 可以用舌前抵紧上齿外,憋住一口气, 形成阻力, 然后用力让气流从舌前和上齿间摩擦成一个相似于普通话拼音中的 "s" 音.与普通话拼音中的 "s" 音不相同之处在于,要让舌前抵紧上齿外,让气流从舌前和上齿间摩擦发出 [θ] 音.

发音结束时,舌前仍然抵上齿外,舌前不要离开上齿外.它是清辅音.

发音三要素	1. 唇势: 扁　　　　　2. 齿距: 舌的厚度 3. 舌位: 舌前抵紧上齿外

32. [ð] 舌前 - 上齿外摩擦音

[θ] 和 [ð] 是一对清,浊辅音. [ð] 发音时, 舌前抵紧上齿外,憋住一口气, 形成阻力, 然后让气流从舌前和上齿间冲出,摩擦成音.发音时,口腔部位与发 [θ] 音的口腔部位相同.普通话中没有 [ð] 音,你可以用舌前抵紧上齿外,憋住一口气, 形成阻力, 然后用力让气流从舌前和上齿间摩擦成一个相似于普通话拼音中的 "r" 音,但与普通话拼音中的 "r" 音不相同. 普通话拼音中的 "r" 音是卷舌音,而国际音标 [ð] 却不能卷舌.发音时,要让舌前抵紧上齿外,让气流从舌前和上齿间摩擦才能发出 [ð] 音.发音结束时,舌前仍然抵上齿外,舌前不要离开上齿外.它是浊辅音.

发音三要素	1. 唇势: 扁　　　　　2. 齿距: 舌的厚度 3. 舌位: 舌前抵紧上齿外

33. [ʃ] 舌中 - 硬颚摩擦音

[ʃ] 和 [ʒ] 是一对清,浊辅音. [ʃ] 发音时, 舌中和硬颚靠近, 但要有间隙.此时, 憋住一口气, 形成阻力, 舌不能卷, 要平伸于口中, 不能碰到上齿和下齿, 然后让气流从舌中和硬颚间冲出, 摩擦成音.在发音时, 口腔部位与下面的 [ʒ] 的发音口腔部位相同.由于普通话中没有 [ʃ] 音,需要让舌中和硬颚靠近, 但要有间隙.此时, 憋住一口气, 形成阻力, 然后用力让气流从舌中和硬颚间摩擦成一个相似于普通话拼音中的 "sh" 音. 但与普通话拼音中 "sh" 音不相同.普通话拼音中 "sh" 音是卷舌音. 而 [ʃ] 却不能卷舌.要领是让舌中和硬颚靠近, 但要有间隙, 让气流从舌中和硬颚间摩擦才能发出 [ʃ] 音. 发音结束时, 舌中和硬颚间仍然有空隙,保持发音时口型, 不要闭嘴.它是清辅音.

发音三要素	1. 唇势: 圆　　　　　2. 齿距: 几乎闭合 3. 舌位: 平伸于口中

34. [ʒ] 舌中 - 硬颚摩擦音	
[ʃ] 和 [ʒ] 是一对清,浊辅音.[ʒ] 发音时,舌中和硬颚靠近,但有间隙,此时,憋住一口气,形成阻力,舌不能卷,要平伸于口中,不能碰到上齿和下齿,然后让气流从舌中和硬颚间冲出,摩擦成音.在发音时,口腔部位与发 [ʃ] 音口腔部位相同.由于普通话中没有 [ʒ] 音,需要让舌中和硬颚靠近,但要有间隙.此时,憋住一口气,形成阻力,然后用力让气流从舌中和硬颚间摩擦成一个相似于普通话拼音中的"r"音.但与普通话拼音中的"r"音不相同.普通话拼音中的"r"音是卷舌音,而国际音标 [ʒ] 却不能卷舌.要领是让舌中和硬颚靠近,但要有间隙,让气流从舌中和硬颚间摩擦才能发出 [ʒ] 音.发音结束时,舌中和硬颚间仍然有空隙,保持发音时的口型,不要闭嘴.它是浊辅音.	
发音三要素	1. 唇势: 圆 2. 齿距: 几乎闭合 3. 舌位: 平伸于口中

35. [h] 声门摩擦音	
发音时,用声门挡住气流,此时,憋住一口气,形成阻力,不能卷舌,要平伸于口中,不能碰到上齿和下齿,然后让气流从声门冲出,摩擦成音.[h]音与普通话中的"喝"的声母音相似,但不相同.要去掉"喝"的声母音的尾音,还要让气流从声门冲出,摩擦成 [h] 音.发音结束时,可以松口气,但是要保持发音时的口型,不要闭嘴.它是清辅音.	
发音三要素	1. 唇势: 扁 2. 齿距: 一个扁指 3. 舌位: 平伸于口中

36. [j] 舌前 - 硬颚摩擦音	
发音时,舌前和硬颚间有空隙,此时,憋住一口气,形成阻力,舌尖抵下齿.嘴唇是扁的,上下牙齿几乎闭合,然后让气流从舌前和硬颚间冲出,摩擦成音.[j]音与普通话中"耶"的声母音相似,但不相同.要去掉"耶"的声母音的尾音,还要让气流从舌前和硬颚间冲出,摩擦成 [j] 音.发音结束时,可松口气,但要保持发音时的口型,不要闭嘴.它是浊辅音.	
发音三要素	1. 唇势: 扁 2. 齿距: 几乎闭合

	3. 舌位: 舌尖抵下齿

37. [w] 舌后-软颚摩擦音	
发音时,舌后和软颚间要有空隙,此时,憋住一口气,形成阻力,不能卷舌, 要平伸于口中,不能碰到上齿和下齿,然后让气流从舌后和软颚间冲出, 摩擦成音. [w] 音与普通话中的"窝"的声母音相似,但不相同.要去掉"窝"的声母音的尾音,还要让气流从舌后和软颚间冲出,摩擦成[w]音.发音结束时,可以松口气,但是要保持发音时的口型,不要闭嘴.它是浊辅音.	
发音三要素	1. 唇势: 圆　　　　2. 齿距: 几乎闭合 3. 舌位: 平伸于口中

38. [r] 舌中 - 硬颚摩擦音	
发音时, 舌中和硬颚间要有空隙,此时,憋住一口气,形成阻力, 不能卷舌, 要平伸于口中, 不要碰到上齿和下齿, 然后让气流从舌中和硬颚间冲出, 摩擦成音. [r] 音与普通话中的 "若" 的声母音相似, 但不相同. "若" 是卷舌音, 是四声, 而国际音标 [r] 却不能卷舌, [r] 是一声. 发音结束时, 可以松口气, 但是要保持发音时的口型, 舌仍然平伸于口中, 不要闭嘴.它是浊辅音.	
发音三要素	1. 唇势: 圆　　　　2. 齿距: 几乎闭合 3. 舌位: 平伸于口中

39. [l] 舌前 - 齿龈舌侧音或旁流音	
辅音字母 l 在单词中发 [l] 音.发音时, 舌尖抵紧上齿龈, 憋住一口气, 形成阻力, 然后让气流从口腔中的舌尖和齿龈两旁突然冲出, 摩擦成 [l] 音.发音时, 口腔部位与发 [t], [d] 和 [n] 音的口腔部位相同. [l] 音与普通话中欧"音相似, 但不相同.发音结束时, 可以松口气, 但是要保持发音时的口型, 舌尖离开上齿龈, 不要闭嘴.它是浊辅音.	
发音三要素	1. 唇势: 扁　　　　2. 齿距: 几乎闭合 3. 舌位: 舌尖抵紧上齿龈

1 [l]
辅音字母 l 在词首或元音前发 [l] 音.发音时,舌尖抵紧上齿龈,憋住一口气,形成阻力,然后让气流从口腔中的舌尖和齿龈两旁突然冲出,摩擦成音.音从舌两旁流出音时,舌尖离开上齿龈.发音时,口腔部位与发 [t], [d] 和 [n] 音的口腔部位相同. [l] 音与普通话中的"了"的声母音相似,但不相同.要去掉"了"的声母音的尾音,还要让气流从口腔中的舌尖和齿龈两旁突然冲出,摩擦成 [l] 音去拼后面的元音.发音结束时,可以松口气,但是要保持发音时的口型,舌尖离开上齿龈,不要闭嘴.它是浊辅音.

发音三要素	1. 唇势: 扁　　　2. 齿距: 几乎闭合
	3. 舌位: 舌尖抵紧上齿龈,音从舌两旁流出音后,舌尖离开上齿龈

40. [m] 双唇-鼻音
辅音字母 m 在单词中发 [m] 音.发音时,双唇紧闭,憋住一口气,不能卷舌,要平伸于口中,不能碰到上齿和下齿,也不能让气流从口腔中出来,要让气流从鼻腔发出 [m] 音.发音时,口腔部位与发 [p] 和 [b] 音的口腔部位相同. [m] 音与普通话中的"牡"的声母音的一声音相似,而"牡"音在普通话中是三声音,但与"牡"的声母音不相同.要去掉"牡"的声母音的尾音,还要双唇紧闭,憋住一口气,让气流从鼻腔发出 [m] 音.发音结束时,可以松口气,但是要保持发音时的口型,不要张开口.它是浊辅音.

发音三要素	1. 唇势: 双唇紧闭　　　2. 齿距: 几乎闭合
	3. 舌位: 平伸于口中

m [m]
辅音字母 m 在词首或元音前发 [m] 音发音时,双唇紧闭,憋住一口气,不能卷舌,要平伸于口中,不能碰到上齿和下齿,也不能让气流从口腔

中出来.要让气流从鼻腔发出 [m] 音. 发音时, 口腔部位与发 [p] 和 [b] 音的口腔部位相同. [m] 在拼它后边的元音时,它的音与普通话拼音中的 "m" 音相似,但要去掉 "m" 音的尾音,还要双唇紧闭,憋住一口气,让气流从鼻腔发出 [m] 音来拼它后面的元音.它是浊辅音.

| 发音三要素 | 1. 唇势: 双唇紧闭 2. 齿距: 几乎闭合 3. 舌位: 平伸于口中 |

41. [n] 舌前-齿龈鼻音

辅音字母 n 在单词中发 [n] 音.发音时, 舌尖抵紧上齿龈, 憋住一口气, 形成阻力, 不能让气流从口腔中出来, 要让气流从鼻腔中发出 [n] 音. 发音时, 口腔部位与发 [t], [d] 和 [l] 音的口腔部位相同. [n] 音与普通话中的 "呢" 的声母音相似, 但不相同, 要去掉 "呢" 的声母音的尾音, 还要舌尖抵紧上齿龈, 憋住一口气, 形成阻力, 让气流从鼻腔中发出 [n] 音.发音结束时, 可以松口气, 但是要保持发音时的口型, 不要闭嘴.舌尖不要离开上齿龈.它是浊辅音.

| 发音三要素 | 1. 唇势: 扁 2. 齿距: 几乎闭合 3. 舌位: 舌尖抵紧上齿龈 |

n [n]

辅音字母 n 在词首或元音前发 [n] 音. 发音时, 舌尖抵紧上齿龈, 憋住一口气, 形成阻力, 不能让气流从口腔中出来, 要让气流从鼻腔中发出 [n] 音.发音时, 口腔部位与发 [t], [d] 和 [l] 音的口腔部位相同. [n] 在拼它后边的元音时, 它的音与普通话拼音中的"n"音相似, 但要去掉 "n" 音的尾音,还要舌尖抵紧上齿龈, 憋住一口气, 形成阻力, 让气流从鼻腔中发出 [n] 音来拼它后边的元音.它是浊辅音.

| | 1. 唇势: 扁 2. 齿距: 几乎闭合 3. 舌位: 舌尖抵紧上齿龈 |

42. [ŋ] 舌后-软颚鼻音	
发音时, 舌跟贴近软颚, 憋住一口气, 形成阻力, 不能让气流从口腔中出来, 要让气流从鼻腔中发出 [ŋ] 音. 发音时, 口腔部位与发 [k] 和 [g] 音的口腔部位相同. [ŋ] 音与普通话拼音中的 "ing" 音的尾音相似, 但不相同.得让你的舌跟贴近软颚, 憋住一口气, 形成阻力, 让气流从鼻腔中发出 [ŋ] 音.发音结束时, 可以松口气, 但是要保持发音时的口型, 不要闭嘴.舌跟和软颚间仍然有空隙.它是浊辅音.	
发音三要素	1. 唇势: 扁　　　　　2. 齿距: 半个扁指 3. 舌位: 舌跟贴近软颚

43. [tr] 破擦音 (既有爆破音又有摩擦音)	
[tr] 和 [dr] 是一对清, 浊辅音.发 [tr] 音时, 舌尖抵紧上齿龈, 憋住一口气, 形成阻力, 然后发 [t] 音, 但不要发出 [t] 音, 就发 [r] 音, 使之摩擦成 [tr] 音.发音时, 口腔部位与发 [dr] 音的口腔部位相同. [tr] 音与普通话中的 "戳" 音相似, 但不相同.普通话中的 "戳" 是卷舌音, 而 [tr] 却不能有卷舌音.要领是破擦音 [tr] 中的[t]音要不完全爆破, 而 [r] 音却要摩擦.发音结束时, 可以松口气, 但是舌仍然平伸于口中, 不要闭嘴.它是清辅音.	
发音三要素	1. 唇势: 圆　　　　　2. 齿距: 几乎闭合 3. 舌位: 首先舌尖抵紧上齿龈, 然后舌中和硬颚间有空隙.

44. [dr] 破擦音 (既有爆破音又有摩擦音)	
[tr] 和 [dr] 是一对清,浊辅音. [dr] 发音时, 舌尖抵紧上齿龈, 憋住一口气, 形成阻力, 然后发 [d] 音, 但不要发出 [d] 音, 就发 [r] 音, 使之摩擦成 [dr] 音.发音时, 口腔部位与发 [tr] 音的口腔部位相同. [dr] 音与普通话中的 "桌" 音相似, 但不相同.普通话中的 "桌" 是卷舌音, 而 [dr] 却不能有卷舌音.要领是破擦音 [dr] 中的 [d] 音要不完	

全爆破, 而 [r] 音却要摩擦.发音结束时, 可以松口气, 但是舌仍然平伸于口中, 不要闭嘴.它是浊辅音.	
发音三要素	1. 唇势: 圆　　　　　　2. 齿距: 几乎闭合 3. 舌位: 首先舌尖抵紧上齿龈, 然后舌中和硬颚间有空隙.

45. [ts] 破擦音 (既有爆破音又有摩擦音)	
[ts] 和 [dz] 是一对清, 浊辅音. [ts] 发音时, 舌尖抵紧上齿龈, 憋住一口气, 形成阻力, 然后让你的舌头顺着上齿龈一直刮止下牙齿摩擦成 [ts] 音.发音时, 口腔部位与发 [dz] 音的口腔部位相同. [ts] 音与普通话拼音中的 "c" 音相似, 但不相同.要领是破擦音 [ts] 中的[t]音要不完全爆破, 而 [s] 音却要摩擦.发音结束时, 舌尖仍然抵下齿, 舌尖不要离开下齿.它是清辅音.	
发音三要素	1. 唇势: 扁　　　　　　2. 齿距: 几乎闭合 3. 舌位: 舌尖抵紧上齿龈, 然后舌头顺着上齿龈一直止下牙齿摩擦成音

46. [dz] 破擦音 (既有爆破音又有摩擦音)	
[ts] 和 [dz] 是一对清, 浊辅音. [dz] 发音时, 舌尖抵紧上齿龈, 憋住一口气, 形成阻力, 然后用舌头顺着上齿龈一直刮止下牙齿摩擦成 [dz] 音.发音时, 口腔部位与发 [ts] 音的口腔部位相同. [dz] 音与普通话拼音中的 "z" 音相似, 但不相同.要领是破擦音 [dz] 中的 [d] 音要不完全爆破, 而 [z] 音却要摩擦.发音结束时, 舌尖仍然抵下齿, 舌尖不要离开下齿.它是浊辅音.	
发音三要素	1. 唇势: 扁　　　　　　2. 齿距: 几乎闭合 3. 舌位: 舌尖抵紧上齿龈, 然后舌头顺着上齿龈一直止下牙齿摩擦成音

47. [tʃ] 破擦音（既有爆破音又有摩擦音）	
[tʃ] 和 [dʒ] 是一对清,浊辅音. [tʃ] 发音时,舌尖抵紧上齿龈,憋住一口气,形成阻力,然后发 [t] 音,但不要发出 [t] 音,就发 [ʃ] 音,使之摩擦成 [tʃ] 音.发音时,口腔部位与发 [dʒ] 音的口腔部位相同. [tʃ] 音与普通话拼音中的 "ch" 音相似,但不相同.普通话拼音中的 "ch" 是卷舌音,而 [tʃ] 却不能有卷舌音.要领是破擦音 [tʃ] 中的 [t] 音要不完全爆破,而 [ʃ] 音却要摩擦.发音结束时,可以松口气,但是舌仍然要平伸于口中,不要闭嘴.它是清辅音.	
发音三要素	1. 唇势: 圆　　　　　　2. 齿距: 几乎闭合 3. 舌位: 首先舌尖抵紧上齿龈,然后舌中和硬颚间要空隙

48. [dʒ] 破擦音（既有爆破音又有摩擦音）	
[tʃ] 和 [dʒ] 是一对清,浊辅音. [dʒ] 发音时,舌尖抵紧上齿龈,憋住一口气,形成阻力,然后发 [d] 音,但不要发出 [d] 音,就发 [ʒ] 音,使之摩擦成 [dʒ] 音.发音时,口腔部位与发 [tʃ] 音的口腔部位相同. [dʒ] 音与普通话拼音中的 "zh" 音相似,但不相同.普通话拼音中的 "zh" 是卷舌音,而 [dʒ] 却不能有卷舌音.要领是破擦音 [dʒ] 中的 [d] 音要不完全爆破,而 [ʒ] 音却要摩擦.发音结束时,可以松口气,但是舌仍然要平伸于口中,不要闭嘴.它是浊辅音.	
发音三要素	1. 唇势: 圆　　　　　　2. 齿距: 几乎闭合 3. 舌位: 首先舌尖抵紧上齿龈,然后舌中和硬颚间要空隙

发音的三要素: 唇势 齿距 舌位

中国新移民学英语语音阶段要牢记的座右铭: 48 个国际音标与中文的发音,虽然有相似的音,但是没有一个是相同的音. 所以,发英语的每个音素都要按发音的三要素去检验.

元音音素的常用读音规则练习表

1. [i:]

be	he	me	she	we
cede	eve	gene	mete	theme
thirteen	fourteen	fifteen	sixteen	seventeen
each	east	eat	eager	easy
flea	lea	pea	sea	tea
beat	heat	lead	meat	team
bee	gee	see	free	knee
beef	feel	need	sheet	week
chief	field	niece	piece	yield
ceiling	receipt	receive		
key				

2. [i]

if	ill	in	is	it
big	disc	fill	film	will
in	inch	increase	insect	insert
bin	gin	pin	tin	win
coin	join	loin	point	ruin
gym	gyp	lynx	myth	nymph
market	harvest	before	device	report
unit	notice	permit	mistake	important
baby	candy	fully	happy	party
certain	curtain	birthday	Friday	Sunday
forfeit	surfeit	money	donkey	monkey
coffee	toffee	cookie	loonie	movie
active	effective	native	relative	sensitive
artist	capitalist	chemist	scientist	socialist

capitalism	hedonism	modernism	optimism	socialism
biscuit	circuit			
dormitory	factory	laboratory	territory	victory
secretary				
furniture				
preposition	position	superposition	supposition	transposition
exclusive	expensive	massive	passive	suspensive
baggage	bandage	garbage	passage	village
minute				

3. [e]

bed	desk	felt	let	met
echo	edge	effort	egg	empty
end	enter	pen	ten	send
bread	head	thread	measure	weather
said				
says				

4. [æ]

bad	dad	hat	sad	tap
act	am	as	at	axe
an	and	fan	van	hand

5. [ʌ]

bus	dust	just	luck	much
ugly	Umm	up	us	utter
under	undress	fun	lunch	punch
brother	dove	honey	love	some
couple	rough	touch	trouble	country
blood	flood			

6. [ə]

ago	banana	comma	central	sofa
purpose	symbol	correct	provide	today
album	campus	circus	upon	support
lunar	solar	motor	Auburn	leader
dangerous	continuous	humorous	jealous	nervous
colour	favour	harbour	labour	neighbour
excellent	president	resident	student	excellent
possible	terrible	holiday	festival	
basement	improvement	judgment	payment	statement
Finland	Ireland	Island	New Zealand	Scotland
furniture	lecture	picture	nature	structure
patience	patient			
electrician	musician	technician	magician	physician
education	instruction	nation	position	preposition
collision	decision	occasion	television	vision
artificial	social	special	specially	specialty
martial	partial			
Asia	Russia			
leisure	measure	pleasure		
brother	weather	leather	mother	father
delicious				
camel	happen	towel		

7. [ə:]

burn	fur	hurt	purl	turn
berth	germ	merge	per	term
bird	birth	dirt	first	third
word	work	world	worm	worth
early	earn	earth	learn	year

| journal | journalist | journey | journalism | |

8. [ɑ:]

bar	car	jar	far	tar
arc	arch	ark	arm	art
dark	farm	hard	park	part
aft	after	aftermath	afternoon	afterthought
answer	dance	glance	plant	slant
ask	cask	flask	mask	task
gasp	grasp	hasp	rasp	raspberry
class	glass	pass	grass	brass
fast	last	mast	past	vast
calf	half	palm		
guano	suave			
Ah				

9. [ɔ]

odd	off	ops	opt	Oscar
boss	dock	fog	pot	sock
on	bond	fond	monk	pond
wand	want	wash	watch	water
cough				
bookshop	dialogue			

10. [ɔ:]

or	orb	order	organ	oral
born	for	lord	port	sort
war	ward	warm	warn	wart
bore	core	fore	more	store
bored	boring	glorious	glory	story

Auburn	August	cause	parse	Paul
awful	draw	law	lawn	saw
ball	call	fall	hall	tall
balk	chalk	talk	walk	calk
caught	naught	taught	Haught	Vaught
boar	board	soar	goar	hoar
caught	naught	taught	Haught	Vaught
boar	board	soar	goar	hoar
door	floor			
court	four	your	pour	yours
bought	fought	thought	brought	sought
born	porn	corn	horn	lorn

11. [u]

book	brook	cook	look	took
foot	good	stood	wood	wool
bathroom	bedroom	classroom	dining-room	washroom
could	should	would		
bush	pull	push	put	bull
beautiful	wonderful	helpful	graceful	joyful

12. [u:]

food	loose	pool	roof	room
balloon	boon	moon	noon	soon
judo	July	June	junior	jute
blue	clue	flue	glue	slue
rule	ruler	rune	true	
flew	grew	Jew	Jewelry	threw
do	to			
lose	move	prove	shoe	movement

who	whom	whose		
fruit	juice	juicy	sluice	ruin
group	mousse	soup	route	
through				
February	century			

13. [e i]

ace	age	ale	ape	ate
gate	face	grape	page	sale
bay	day	gay	pay	say
aid	aim	mail	rain	gain
gain	main	pain	rain	plain
break	great	steak		
veil	vein	gein	beige	feint
hey	obey	they	bey	dey
eight	freight	neighbour	weigh	weight
straight				
baby	famous	later	nation	table
generate	separate	eliminate	accelerate	calculate

14. [a i]

I	Hi	ice	bi	pi
bike	side	tide	hide	five
by	my	shy	cry	why
type	dyke	dike	byte	tyke
light	night	sight	fight	might
child	mild	wild		
bind	find	hind	kind	mind
fine	line	mine	nine	pine
bye	dye	eye	lye	rye

die	lie	pie	tie	
guide	guidance			
buy	guy			
height				
climb				
ninth				
aisle				
apologize	appetite	exercise	modernize	organize
certify	identify	qualify	satisfy	verify

15. [a u]

ouch	oust	out	outdoors	outer
cloud	loud	proud	mouth	south
blouse	house	mouse	spouse	douse
around	found	pound	round	sound
account	bounce	count	ounce	pronounce
how	now	power	tower	wow
down	downstairs	download	downs	downtown
town	town-hall	townhouse	township	uptown
brown	clown	crown	drown	frown
doughty	drought	plough	sough	bough

16. [ə u]

O	go	no	so	po
ode	ope	oke		
globe	lone	sole	stone	zone
oak	coat	coast	load	road
doe	foe	hoe	Joe	toe
bow	grow	low	slow	tow

new	sew	dew	few	hew
bolt	volt	dolt	molt	holt
folk	folksy	yolk	folklore	
old	fold	gold	sold	bold
roll	stroll	toll	boll	poll
host	most	post	ghost	
dough	doughnut	though	although	
also	photo	yellow	mango	fellow
don't	won't			
both	loth			
only				
own				
Hello	Oh	OK		

17. [ɔi]

oil	boil	foil	soil	spoil
appointment	coin	join	joint	point
choice	foist	noise	voice	void
boy	coy	joy	soy	toy
annoy	destroy	employ	employee	enjoy

18. [iə]

here	mere	sere	sincere	sphere
experience	material	period	serious	glorious
clear	dear	fear	hear	near
beer	career	cheer	deer	leer
bier	cashier	frontier	pier	premier
weird	weir	seir		
peon	peony	theory	theorem	theoretical
Claudia	Julia	Maria	Sophia	Victoria

billion	million	onion	union	trillion
auditorium	medium	stadium s	odium	
museum				
engineer	pioneer	volunteer		

19. [εə]

care	dare	fare	hare	share
variable	various	vary	wary	area
chair	fair	hair	pair	stair
bear	pear	swear	tear	wear
there	thereafter	thereby	therefore	where
their	theirs	heir	Meir	Neir

20. [uə]

dour	gourd	gourmand	gourmet	tour
boor	moor	poor	Bloor	Noor
lure	sure	dure		
juror	jury	plural	prurient	rural

21. [aiə]

fire	hire	spire	tire	wire
firing	hirable	miry	siren	spiral
dial	dialect	dialogue	diameter	diamond
pioneer	pious	lion	violet	violin
client	diet	quiet		
bias	biased			
flyer	plyer	fryer	pryer	cryer
cyanide	cyan	cyanosis	cyaniding	cyanuric

22. [auə]

our	flour	hour	lour	sour
flower	power	tower	bower	cower
towel	bowel	vowel	dowel	howel
nowadays				
flour				

23. [ɔ i ə]

enjoyable	loyal	royal	soya bean	soya sauce
employer	foyer			
joyous				
doyen				
coir				

元音音素的常用读音规则练习表 (附带说明)

1. [i:]

be	he	me	开音节
cede	eve	gene	开音节
thirteen	fourteen	fifteen	teen [ti :n]
each	east	eat	ea _ [i:]
flea	lea	pea	_ ea [i:]
beat	heat	lead	_ ea _ [i:]
bee	gee	see	_ ee [i:]
beef	feel	need	_ ee _ [i:]
chief	field	niece	ie [i:]
ceiling	receipt	receive	ei [i:]
key			ey [i:]

2. [i]

if	ill	in	i -闭音节 [i]
big	disc	fill	i -闭音节 [i]
in	inch	increase	in _ [in]
bin	gin	pin	_ in [in]
coin	join	loin	_ in [in]
gym	gyp	lynx	y -闭音节
market	harvest	before	在非重读音节中[i]
unit	notice	permit	i 在非重读音节中[i]
baby	candy	fully	在非重读音节中[i]
certain	curtain	birthday	在非重读音节中[i]
forfeit	surfeit	money	ey 在非重读音节中[i]
coffee	toffee	cookie	ie 在非重读音节中[i]
active	effective	native	_ tive [tiv]
artist	capitalist	chemist	_ ist [ist]

capitalism	hedonism	modernism	_ ism [izm]
biscuit	circuit		ui 在非重读音节中[i]
dormitory	factory	laboratory	ui 在非重读音节中[i]
secretary			_ tary [tri]
furniture			_ iture [itʃə]
preposition	position	supposition	_ ition [iʃən]
division	provision	revision	_ ision [iʒən]
exclusive	expensive	massive	_ sive [siv]
baggage	bandage	garbage	age 读[idʒ]
minute			_ u [i]

3. [e]

bed	desk	felt	e -闭音节[e]
echo	edge	effort	词首的[e]
end	enter	pen	e -闭音节[e]
bread	head	thread	ea [e]
said			ai [e]
says			ay [e]

4. [æ]

bad	dad	hat	a - 闭音节[æ]
act	am	as	词首的[æ]
an	and	fan	词中的[æ]

5. [ʌ]

bus	dust	just	u - 闭音节[ʌ]
ugly	umm	up	utter 词首的[ʌ]
under	undress	fun	_ un [ʌ]
brother	dove	honey	_ o [ʌ]
couple	rough	touch	_ ou [ʌ]

blood	flood		_ oo [ʌ]

6. [ə]

ago	banana	comma	a 在非重读音节中[ə]
purpose	symbol	correct	o 在非重读音节中[ə]
album	campus	circus	u 在非重读音节中[ə]
lunar	solar	motor	_ ar, or, ur, er [ə]
dangerous	continuous	humorous	_ ous [əs]
colour	favour	harbour	_ our [ə]
excellent	president	resident	_ ent [ənt]
possible	terrible	holiday	i 在非重读音节中[ə]
basement	improvement	judgment	_ ment [mənt]
Finland	Ireland	Island	_ land [lənd]
furniture	lecture	picture	_ ture [tʃə]
patience	patient		_ tien [ʃən]
electrician	musician	technician	_ cian [ʃən]
education	instruction	nation	_ tion [ʃən]
collision	decision	occasion	_ sion [ʒən]
artificial	social	special	_ cial [ʃəl]
martial	partial		_tial [ʃəl]
Asia	Russia		_sia [ʃə]
leisure	measure	pleasure	_ sure [ʒə]
brother	weather	feather	_ ther [ðə]
delicious			_cious [ʃəs]
camel	happen	towel	e 在非重读音节中[ə]

7. [ə:]

burn	fur	hurt	u r 在 R 音节中 [ə:]
berth	germ	merge	e r 在 R 音节中 [ə:]
bird	birth	dirt	i r 在 R 音节中 [ə:]

word	work	world	wor [ə:]
early	earn	earth	ear [ə:]
journal	journalist	journey	our [ə:]

8. [ɑ:]

bar	car	jar	a r 在 R 音节中 [ɑ:]
arc	arch	ark	a r 在 R 音节中 [ɑ:]
dark	farm	hard	a r 在 R 音节中 [ɑ:]
aft	after	aftermath	aft [ɑ:f t]
answer	dance	glance	an [ɑ: n]
ask	cask	flask	ask [ɑ:sk]
gasp	grasp	hasp	Asp [ɑ:sp]
class	glass	pass	Ass [ɑ:s]
fast	last	past	Ast [ɑ:st]
calf	half	palm	al [ɑ:]
Ah			[ɑ:]

9. [ɔ]

odd	off	Oscar	o 在闭音节中 [ɔ]
boss	dock	fog	o 在闭音节中 [ɔ]
on	bond	fond	on [ɔn]
wand	want	wash	wa [w ɔ]
cough			ou [ɔ]
bookshop	dialogue		o 在非重读音节中 [ɔ]

10. [ɔ:]

or	orb	order	o r 在 R 音节中 [ɔ:]
born	for	lord	o r 在 R 音节中 [ɔ:]
war	ward	warm	war [w ɔ:]
bore	core	fore	ore [ɔ:]

bored	boring	glorious	or + 元音字母 [ɔ: r]
Auburn	August	cause	au [ɔ:]
awful	draw	law	aw [ɔ:]
ball	call	fall	all [ɔ: l]
almost	already	also	al [ɔ: l]
balk	chalk	talk	al [ɔ:]
caught	naught	taught	augh [ɔ:]
boar	board	soar	oar [ɔ:]
door	floor		oor [ɔ:]
court	four	your	our [ɔ:]
bought	fought	thought	ough [ɔ:]
born	porn	corn	orn [ɔ: n]

11. [u]

book	brook	cook	oo 在 k 前 [u]
foot	good	stood	oo [u]
bathroom	classroom	dining-room	oo 在合成词中 [u]
could	should	would	oul [u]
bush	pull	push	u [u]
beautiful	joyful	wonderful	ful [ful]

12. [u:]

food	loose	pool	oo [u:]
balloon	boon	moon	oon [u: n]
judo	July	June	u 在 j 后 [u:]–开音节
blue	clue	flue	u 在 l 后 [u:]–开音节
rule	ruler	rune	u 在 r 后 [u:]–开音节
flew	grew	Jew	ew [u:]
do	to		o [u:]
lose	move	prove	o [u:]

who	whom	whose	o [u:]
fruit	juice	sluice	ui [u:]
group	mousse	soup	ou [u:]
through			ough [u:]
February	century		u [u:]

13. [e i]

ace	age	ale	a 在开音节中 [e i]
gate	face	grape	a 在开音节中 [e i]
bay	day	gay	ay [e i]
aid	aim	mail	ai [e i]
gain	main	pain	ain [e i n]
break	great	steak	ea [e i]
veil	vein	gein	ei [e i]
hey	obey	they	ey [e i]
eight	freight	neighbour	eigh [e i]
straight			aigh [e i]
baby	famous	later	a 在开音节中 [e i]
generate	separate	eliminate	ate [e i t]

14. [a i]

I	Hi	ice	i 在开音节中 [ai]
bike	side	tide	i 在开音节中 [ai]
by	my	shy	y 开音节中 [ai]
type	dyke	dike	y 开音节中 [ai]
light	night	sight	igh [ai]
child	mild	wild	[aild]
bind	find	hind	ind[aind]
fine	line	mine	i 在开音节中 [ai]
bye	dye	eye	ye [ai]

die	lie	pie	ie [ai]
guide	guidance		ui [ai]
buy	guy		uy [ai]
height			eigh [ai]
climb			i 在闭音节中 [ai]
ninth			i 在闭音节中 [ai]
aisle			ai [ai]
apologize	appetite	modernize	i 在非重读音节中 [ai]
certify	identify	qualify	y 在非重读音节中 [ai]

15. [a u]

ouch	oust	out	ou [a u]
cloud	loud	proud	ou [a u]
blouse	house	mouse	ou [a u]
around	found	pound	oun [aun]
account	bounce	ount	oun [aun]
how	now	power	ow [a u]
down	downstairs	download	own [aun]
town	town-hall	townhouse	own [aun]
brown	clown	crown	own [aun]
doughty	drought	plough	ough [a u]

16. [ə u]

go	no	so	o 在开音节中 [ə u]
ode	ope	oke	o 在开音节中 [ə u]
globe	lone	sole	o 在开音节中 [ə u]
oak	coat	coast	oa [ə u]
doe	foe	hoe	oe [ə u]
bow	grow	low	ow [ə u]
new	sew	dew	ew [ə u]

bold	bolt	volt	olt [əult]
folk	folksy	yolk	olk [əulk]
old	fold	gold	old [əuld]
roll	stroll	toll	oll [əul]
host	most	post	ost [əust]
dough	doughnut	though	ough [əu]
photo	yellow	also	在非重读音节中 [əu]
don't	won't		ont [əu]
both	loth		o 在闭音节中 [əu]
only			o 在闭音节中 [əu]
own			o 在闭音节中 [əu]
Hello	Oh	OK	o 在感叹词中 [əu]

17. [ɔi]

oil	boil	foil	oi [ɔi]
coin	join	joint	oi [ɔi]
choice	foist	noise	oi [ɔi]
boy	coy	joy	oy [ɔi]
annoy	destroy	employ	oy [ɔi]

18. [iə]

here	mere	sere	ere [iə]
experience	material	period	er +元音字母 [iər]
clear	dear	fear	ear [iə]
beer	career	cheer	eer [iə]
bier	cashier	frontier	eir [iə]
weird	weir	seir	eir [iə]
peon	peony	theory	eo [iə]
Claudia	Julia	Maria	ia [iə]
billion	million	onion	io [iə]

auditorium	medium	stadium	iu [iə]
museum			eu [iə]
engineer	pioneer	volunteer	eer [iə]

19. [ɛə]

care	dare	fare	[ɛə]
variable	various	vary	ar+元音字母[ɛər]
chair	fair	hair	air [ɛə]
bear	pear	swear	ear [ɛə]
there	thereafter	thereby	ere [ɛə]
their	theirs	heir	eir [ɛə]

20. [uə]

dour	gourd	gourmand	our [uə]
boor	moor	poor	oor [uə]
lure	sure	dure	ure [uə]
juror	jury	plural	ur+元音字母[uər]

21. [aiə]

fire	hire	spire	ire [aiə]
firing	hirable	miry	ir +元音字母[aiər]
dial	dialect	violin	io [aiə]
client	diet	quiet	ie [aiə]
bias	biased		ia [aiə]
flyer	plyer	fryer	yer [aiə]
cyanide	cyan	cyanosis	ya [aiə]

22. [auə]

our	flour	hour	our [auə]
flower	power	tower	ower [auə]

towel	bowel	vowel	owe [auə]
nowadays			owa [auə]
flour			our [auə]

23. [ɔi ə]

enjoyable	loyal	royal	oya [ɔi ə]
employer	foyer		oyer [ɔi ə]
joyous			oyou [ɔi ə]
doyen			oye [ɔi ə]
coir			oir [ɔi ə]

辅音音素的常用读音规则练习表

1. [p]

pave	Pea	pie	pig	pipe
leap	lip	peep	ship	shop
tape	hope	pipe	ripe	type
pack	pet	pick	pot	pub
park	per	pork	port	purse
plan	plant	play	please	plus
pray	press	price	proof	proud
happy	poppy	supper	shopper	topping
apple	topple	couple	dimple	simple

2. [b]

bake	back	bark	bare	bee
club	Lab.	rib	rob	pub
break	brief	bright	bring	broom
bobby	Debby	hobby	lobby	rabbit
bubble	rabble	able	double	trouble

3. [t]

take	tip	tar	tire	team
bit	fit	sit	meat	smart
bite	cite	mite	rite	site
twenty	twice	twig	twist	twin
little	kettle	settle	title	turtle

4. [d]

date	did	dark	dare	deep
deed	lead	need	paid	stand

blade	grade	made	ride	tide
middle	riddle	kindle	needle	noodle

5. [k]

kite	kick	kart	keep	kind
bank	mink	rank	sink	think
back	pack	pick	sick	tick
box	fix	fox	mix	six
cake	cost	car	care	caution
cap	code	cost	cut	cute
arctic	athletic	clinic	disc	Mac
chemical	Christ	headache	school	technology
class	clean	clear	close	club
craft	cream	crowd	crown	cry
bicycle	cycle	pickle	uncle	ankle
queen	quick	quit	quite	quest
excellent	exchange	excuse	exit	exhibition

6. [g]

gap	gate	go	got	gum
game	gas	girl	gore	gory
dig	dog	fog	log	pig
bigger	digger	egg	foggy	jogger
boggle	giggle	straggle	struggle	wriggle
dingle	google	jingle	mingle	single
glad	glance	glass	glen	globe
grace	grade	grain	grass	green
ghastly	ghee	ghetto	ghost	ghoul
gift	gig	gild	gill	gilt
gird	girl	girt	girth	girdle

guard	guess	guest	guide	guitar
dialogue	league	fatigue	vague	vogue
exam	example	exist	exhausted	exhibit
configure	figure	disfigure	prefigure	transfigure

7. [f]

file	fine	five	flag	fly
fife	life	knife	rife	wife
buff	cuff	Jeff	off	puff
buffet	coffee	office	different	difficult
cough	enough	laugh	rough	tough
phone	photo	phrase	graph	paragraph
flag	flash	flea	floor	fly
frame	free	fresh	frog	from
baffle	muffle	snuffle	TOEFL	waffle
hyphen	often	orphan	Stephen	stiffen

8. [v]

vale	vane	vest	vote	van
have	live	move	save	valve
driver	liver	never	over	river
arrival	rival			
novel	rival	snivel	travel	
eleven	heaven	oven	proven	seven

9. [s]

space	speak	speed	spell	spit
staff	stage	stair	stamp	stand
skate	skirt	skill	skin	sky
scale	scan	scar	school	score

straw	street	stress	strike	strong
slang	slave	sleep	slice	slow
small	smart	smell	smoke	smooth
snack	snake	snap	snore	snow
square	squash	squeeze	squid	squirrel
swan	sweat	sweet	swipe	switch
ceiling	cell	cent	certain	certificate
cider	cigar	cinema	circle	cite
cycle	cyclic	cyclist	cyclone	cymbal
dance	face	nice	office	place
close	horse	house	use	worse
class	glass	grass	kiss	miss
fasten	lessen	listen	recent	vixen
cancel	muscle	parcel	pencil	tussle
bustle	castle	hustle	jostle	whistle
defensive	expensive	explosive	offensive	passive
artist	chemist	capitalist	socialist	scientist

10. [z]

zebra	zero	zest	zone	zoo
blaze	graze	maze	prize	size
noise	nose	please	these	rise
as	has	is	Ms.	was
buzz	fizz	frizz	fuzz	quiz
frizzle	guzzle	muzzle	puzzle	nozzle
crazy	frenzy	hazy	lazy	woozy
business	busy	dizzy	frizzy	fuzzy

11. [θ]

thank	theme	thick	thigh	third
cloth	mouth	north	south	truth
author	birthday	faithful	nothing	strengthen

12. [ð]

this	that	these	those	though
booth	smooth	with		
withdraw	withhold	within	without	withstand
bathe	breathe	teethe	lathe	soothe
another	brother	either	leather	together
northern	southern			

13. [ʃ]

sharp	sheet	ship	shop	shout
bush	cash	push	wash	wish
caution	education	instruction	occupation	station
exhibition	opposition	position	preposition	tuition
extension	hypertension	pension	suspension	tension
commission	mission	permission	profession	session
chalet	champagne	chef	machine	moustache
Confucian	electrician	musician	physician	technician
artificial	official	racial	special	social
confidential	initial	martial	partial	potential
Asia	Asian	Russia		
efficiency	efficient	fashion	patience	patient
ambitious	contentious	nutritious	ostentatious	pretentious
assure	assured	assuredly	self-assured	reassure
ensure	insure	reinsure	sure	surety
insurance	insurant	reinsurance		

censure	pressure			
sugar	sugary	sugariness	sugar beet	sugar lump
cashier				
ocean				
fashion				

14. [ʒ]

beige	garage	luge		
usual	usually	usurer	usury	
disclosure	exposure	leisure	measure	pleasure
seizure				
confusion	extrusion	occasion	obtrusion	protrusion
collision	decision	division	television	vision
Persian				

15. [h]

hate	hope	huge	he	hide
hat	hot	hut	hen	hid
hard	horn	hurt	herb	hirsute
who	whom	whose	whoever	whole

16. [j]

Yale	ye	yoke	yule	yoga
yak	yellow	yes	yet	yummy
courtyard	yard	York	Yorkshire	Yorker
cure	pure	secure	security	yore
year	yeast	yield	yolk	your
use	usage	useful	useless	user
cute	duke	fuse	puke	tube
dew	few	hew	new	yew

cue	due	fuel	hue	sue

17. [w]

wage	wave	wide	wife	wine
wash	watch	well	will	wish
war	ward	warden	warm	warn
word	work	world	worse	worth
ware	warehouse	wore	were-wolf	wire
walk	way	weak	wear	week
water	waver	wavy	weather	welfare
when	where	why	what	which
while	whim	whip	whistle	white
one	once	anyone	everyone	someone
swan	sweep	sweet	swim	sweater
swan	sweep	sweet	swim	sweater
anguish	language	languid	linguist	penguin

18. [r]

race	rape	rate	ripe	rise
ram	ranch	rat	red	rush
rare	rain	raw	ray	read
arrive	correct	mirror	rasp-beery	strawberry
wrap	wrench	wrestle	wrist	wrong
brake	bring	brief	bridge	brown
clock	crew	crime	cross	cry
frame	free	fresh	fridge	from
grace	grade	green	ground	grow
pray	premier	presentation	president	price
rude	rule	rune	ruse	rupee

19. [l]

late	list	lost	lark	lead
close	fly	glad	slice	slope
bill	cell	dull	pill	till
jilt	kilt	milk	silk	tilt
blade	black	blue	block	bleach
class	clean	clear	close	club
flag	flash	flea	floor	fly
glad	glance	glass	glen	globe
plane	plan	plus	plant	play
almost	already	also	although	always
all	ball	hall	mall	tall
boll	poll	roll	stroll	toll
alike	allow	alone	along	aloud
bolt	dolt	jolt	molt	volt
bold	cold	fold	gold	told
child	mild	wild		
beautiful	faithful	graceful	hopeful	wonderful
bottle	middle	cycle	single	purple
luge	lute	blue	flute	glue

20. [m]

make	mop	mark	mere	mouth
am	from	gum	plum	slim
dime	lime	mime	rime	time
small	smart	smell	smoke	smile
hammer	mummer	simmer	summer	swimmer
Autumn	column			

21. [n]

name	not	nurse	north	near
fine	line	mine	pine	wine
snack	snake	snap	sneeze	snow
knee	knife	knock	know	knuckle
bunny	funny	penny	runny	sunny
christen	fasten	lessen	listen	recent
thirteen	fourteen	fifteen	sixteen	seventeen
inch	input	insect	Linda	pin
end	enter	ten	send	men
an	and	fan	van	hand
under	undress	bun	fun	lunch
answer	dance	plant	glance	slant
on	onto	fond	pond	bond
moon	noon	soon	sooner	goon
round	found	pound	count	mount
campaign	design	designer	foreign	sign

22. [ŋ]

king	ring	sing	thing	wing
along	long	song	strong	wrong
bung	dung	hung	lung	sung
bungle	funky	hungry	punctual	uncle
anger	angle	anglicize	angora	angry
longer	stronger	younger		
longest	strongest	youngest		
bank	hank	rank	tank	thank
funk	hunk	junk	punk	sunk
anger	finger	linger		
ringer	singer	winger		

23. [ts]

cats	hats	lets	tests	sits
dates	gates	hates	plates	states

24. [dz]

beds	hands	leads	stands	words
blades	grades	spades		

25. [tr]

treat	trip	tress	tract	trust
tradition	trance	trot	trauma	troop
true	trade	try	trout	trope
troika				

26. [dr]

dream	drill	dress	drag	drug
dramatic	drama	drop	draw	drew
drake	dry	drought	drone	dreary

27. [tʃ]

chair	chart	cheap	choose	church
bench	lunch	March	much	peach
catch	fetch	match	switch	watch
culture	future	lecture	nature	picture
furniture				
question	questionable	questioner	questionnaire	suggestion

28. [dʒ]

jade	jape	jive	joke	joke
jab	job	jug	jump	just

jar	jargon	jerboa	jerk	jerkin
jaw	jealous	joint	jolly	joy
judo	juke-box	June	July	jute
gee	gem	germ	general	gesture
gibe	gin	ginger	ginseng	gist
age	cage	gage	large	page
badge	bridge	edge	fridge	fudge
baggage	bandage	garbage	passage	village
education	gradually	graduation	individual	procedure
change	exchange	grange	range	orange
messenger	passenger			
college				

English Pronunciation for Chinese Speakers

辅音音素的常用读音规则练习表（附带说明）

1. [p]

pave	pea	pie	pig	在词首
leap	lip	peep	ship	在词尾
tape	hope	pipe	ripe	尾音[p]
pack	pet	pick	pot	闭音节
park	per	pork	port	R 音节
plan	plant	play	please	pl _
pray	press	price	proof	pr _
happy	poppy	supper	shopper	pp
apple	topple	couple	dimple	_ pl

2. [b]

bake	back	bark	bare	在词首
club	lab	rib	rob	在词尾
blade	black	blue	block	bl _
break	brief	bright	bring	br _
bobby	Debby	hobby	lobby	bb
bubble	rabble	able	double	_ bl

3. [t]

take	tip	tar	tire	在词首
bit	fit	sit	meat	在词尾
bite	cite	mite	rite	尾音[t]
twenty	twice	twig	twist	tw _
little	kettle	settle	title	_ tl

4. [d]

date	did	dark	dare	在词首
deed	lead	need	paid	在词尾
blade	grade	made	ride	尾音[d]
middle	riddle	kindle	needle	_ dl

5. [k]

kite	kick	kart	keep	在词首
bank	mink	rank	sink	在词尾
back	pack	pick	sick	_ ck
box	fix	fox	mix	_ x
cake	cost	car	care	(c 在 a, o.
cap	code	cost	cut	u 前, 或其它
arctic	athletic	clinic	disc	场合, 读[k])
chemical	Christ	headache	school	ch [k]
class	clean	clear	close	cl _
craft	cream	crowd	crown	cr _
bicycle	cycle	pickle	uncle	[kl]
antique	brusque	cheque	pique	_ que
queen	quick	quit	quite	qu _
excellent	exchange	excuse	exit	ex _

6. [g]

gap	gate	go	got	在词首
game	gas	girl	gore	在词首
dig	dog	fog	log	在词尾
bigger	digger	egg	foggy	gg
boggle	giggle	straggle	struggle	[gl]
dingle	google	jingle	mingle	[gl]
glad	glance	glass	glen	gl _

grace	grade	grain	grass	gr _
ghastly	ghee	ghetto	ghost	gh [g]
gift	gig	gild	gill	特殊情况
gird	girl	girt	girth	特殊情况
guard	guess	guest	guide	gu [g]
dialogue	league	fatigue	vague	gue
exam	example	exist	exhausted	ex [igz]
configure	disfigure	prefigure	transfigure	gure [gə]

7. [f]

file	fine	five	flag	在词首
fife	life	knife	rife	尾音[f]
buff	cuff	Jeff	off	在词尾
buffet	coffee	office	different	ff
cough	enough	laugh	rough	gh [f]
phone	photo	phrase	graph	ph [f]
flag	flash	flea	floor	fl _
frame	free	fresh	frog	fr _
baffle	muffle	snuffle	TOEFL	[fl]
hyphen	often	orphan	Stephen	[fn]

8. [v]

vale	vane	vest	vote	在词首
have	live	move	save	尾音[v]
driver	liver	never	over	ver
arrival	rival			val
novel	rival	snivel	travel	vel
eleven	heaven	oven	proven	ven

9. [s]

space	speak	speed	spell	sp _
staff	stage	stair	stamp	st _
skate	skirt	skill	skin	sk _
scale	scan	scar	school	sc _
straw	street	stress	strike	str _
slang	slave	sleep	slice	sl _
small	smart	smell	smoke	sm _
snack	snake	snap	snore	sn _
square	squash	squeeze	squid	squ _
swan	sweat	sweet	swipe	sw _
ceiling	cent	certain	certificate	c在e, i, y
cider	cigar	cinema	circle	前, 读 [s]
cycle	cyclic	cyclist	cyclone	
dance	face	nice	office	_ ce [s]
close	horse	house	use	_ se [s]
class	glass	grass	kiss	_ ss [s]
fasten	lessen	listen	recent	[sn]
cancel	muscle	parcel	pencil	[sl]
bustle	castle	hustle	jostle	[sl]
defensive	expensive	explosive	offensive	sive [siv]
artist	chemist	capitalist	socialist	ist [ist]

10. [z]

zebra	zero	zest	zone	在词首
blaze	graze	maze	prize	尾音[z]
noise	nose	please	these	se [z]
as	has	is	Ms.	s [z]
buzz	fizz	frizz	fuzz	在词尾
frizzle	guzzle	muzzle	puzzle	[zl]

crazy	frenzy	hazy	lazy	_ zy [zi]
business	busy	dizzy	frizzy	[zi]

11. [θ]

thank	theme	thick	thigh	在词首
cloth	mouth	north	south	在词尾
author	birthday	faithful	nothing	在词中

12. [ð]

this	that	these	those	在词首
booth	smooth	with		在词尾
withdraw	withhold	within	without	在词中
bathe	breathe	teethe	lathe	_ the [ð]
another	brother	either	leather	_ ther [ðə]
northern	southern			_ thern [ðən]

13. [ʃ]

sharp	sheet	ship	shop	在词首
bush	cash	push	wash	在词尾
caution	education	instruction	occupation	tion [ʃən]
opposition	preposition	tuitionition	exhibition	[iʃən]
hypertension	suspension	tensionsion	extension	[ʃən]
commission	permission	profession	mission	ssion[ʃən]
chalet	champagne	machine	moustache	ch [ʃ]
Confucian	electrician	musician	physician	cian [ʃn]
artificial	official	racial	special	cial [ʃl]
confidential	initial	martial	partial	cial [ʃl]
Asia	Asian	Russia		sia [ʃə]
efficiency	efficient	fashion	patience	[ʃn]
ambitious	contentious	ostentatious	nutritious	[ʃəs]

assure	assuredly	self-assured	assured	[ʃuə]
ensure	insure	reinsure	sure	[ʃuə]
insurance	insurant	reinsurance		[ʃuə]
censure	pressure			[ʃə]
sugar	sugariness	sugar beet	sugary	[ʃuə]
cashier				[ʃiə]
ocean				[ʃn]
fashion				[ʃn]

14. [ʒ]

beige	garage	luge		在词尾
usual	usually	usurer	usury	在词中
disclosure	exposure	measure	pleasure	sure [ʒə]
seizure				zure [ʒə]
confusion	extrusion	occasion	obtrusion	sion [ʒən]
collision	decision	division	television	ision [ʒən]
Persian				sian [ʒən]

15. [h]

hate	hope	huge	he	开音节
hat	hot	hut	hen	闭音节
hard	horn	hurt	herb	R 音节
who	whom	whose	whole	o 在 wh 后[h]

16. [j]

Yale	ye	yoke	yule	开音节
yak	yellow	yes	yet	闭音节
courtyard	yard	York	Yorkshire	R 音节
cure	pure	secure	security	Re 音节
year	yeast	yield	yolk	首音[ju:]

197

U	U. S. A.	U. S. S. R.	U-turn	首音 [ju:]
use	usage	useful	useless	首音 [ju:]
cute	duke	fuse	puke	u 在开音节中
dew	few	hew	new	尾音 [ju:]
cue	due	fuel	hue	尾音 [ju:]

17. [w]

wage	wave	wide	wife	开音节
wash	watch	well	will	闭音节
war	ward	warden	warm	R 音节
word	work	world	worse	R 音节
ware	warehouse	wore	were-wolf	Re 音节
walk	way	weak	wear	字母组合
water	waver	wavy	weather	双音节词
when	where	why	what	疑问词的读音
while	whim	whip	whistle	wh_ 的读音
one	once	anyone	everyone	[w]
swan	sweep	sweet	swim	sw _
twelve	twenty	twice	twin	tw _
anguish	language	languid	linguist	gu [gw]
quality	quarter	quick	quit	qu [kw]

18. [r]

race	rape	rate	ripe	开音节
ram	ranch	rat	red	闭音节
rare	rain	raw	ray	字母组合
carry	hurry	marry	sorry	双 R 音节
arrive	correct	rasp-beery	strawberry	非重读音节
wrap	wrench	wrestle	wrist	wr _
brake	bring	brief	bridge	br _

clock	crew	crime	cross	cr _
frame	free	fresh	fridge	fr _
grace	grade	green	ground	gr _
pray	premier	presentation	president	pr _
rude	rule	rune	ruse	u 在 r 后-开音节

19. [l]

late	list	lost	lark	在词首
close	fly	glad	slice	在元音前
late	list	lost	lark	在词首
close	fly	glad	slice	在元音前
bill	cell	dull	pill	在词尾
jilt	kilt	milk	silk	在词中
blade	black	blue	block	bl _
class	clean	clear	close	cl _
flag	flash	flea	floor	fl _
glad	glance	glass	glen	gl _
plane	plan	plus	plant	pl _
almost	already	also	although	al _
all	ball	hall	mall	all [ɔ:l]
boll	poll	roll	stroll	oll [əul]
alike	allow	alone	along	al _
bolt	dolt	jolt	molt	olt [əult]
bold	cold	fold	gold	old [əuld]
child	mild	wild		ild [aild]
beautiful	faithful	graceful	hopeful	ful [ful]
bottle	middle	cycle	single	[- l]
luge	lute	blue	flute	u 在 l 后-开音节

20. [m]

make	mop	mark	mere	在词首
am	from	gum	plum	在词尾
dime	lime	mime	rime	尾音[m]
small	smart	smell	smoke	sm _
hammer	mummer	simmer	summer	sw _
Autumn	column			_ mn [m]

21. [n]

name	not	nurse	north	在词首
fine	line	mine	pine	尾音[n]
snack	snake	snap	sneeze	在词中[n]
knee	knife	knock	know	kn_ [n]
bunny	funny	penny	runny	[ni]
christen	fasten	lessen	listen	[sn]
thirteen	fourteen	fifteen	sixteen	[i :]
inch	input	insect	Linda	[in]
end	enter	ten	send	[en]
an	and	fan	van	[æn]
under	undress	bun	fun	[ʌn]
answer	dance	plant	glance	[ɑ:nt]
on	onto	fond	pond	[ɔn]
moon	noon	soon	sooner	[u:n]
round	found	pound	count	[aunt]
campaign	design	designer	foreign	gn [n]

22. [ŋ]

king	ring	sing	thing	ing [iŋ]
along	long	song	strong	ong [ɔŋ]
bung	dung	hung	lung	ung [ʌŋ]

bungle	funky	hungry	punctual	un[ʌŋ]
anger	angle	anglicize	angora	ung[æŋg]
longer	stronger	younger	nger	[ŋgə]
longest	strongest	youngest	ngest	[ŋgist]
bank	hank	rank	tank	_ nk[ŋ k]
pink	rink	sink	think	_ ink [iŋk]
funk	hunk	junk	punk	_ unk [ʌŋk]
anger	finger	linger		- nger [ŋgə]
ringer	singer	winger		- nger [ŋgə]

23. [ts]

cats	hats	lets	tests	_ ts [ts]
dates	gates	hates	plates	_ tes [ts]

24. [dz]

beds	hands	leads	stands	_ ds [dz]
blades	grades	spades		_ des [dz]

25. [tr]

treat	trip	tress	tract	tr 拼元音
tradition	trance	trot	trauma	tr 拼元音
true	trade	try	trout	tr 拼元音
Troika				tr 拼元音

26. [dr]

dream	drill	dress	drug	dr 拼元音
dramatic	drama	drop	draw	dr 拼元音
drake	dry	drought	drone	dr 拼元音

27. [tʃ]

chair	chart	cheap	choose	在词首
bench	lunch	March	much	在词尾
catch	fetch	match	switch	tch [tʃ]
culture	future	lecture	nature	ture [tʃə]
furniture				iture [itʃə]
question	questionable	questioner	suggestion	stion [stʃən]

28. [dʒ]

jade	jape	jive	joke	j-开音节
jab	job	jug	jump	j-闭音节
jar	jargon	jerboa	jerk	j-R 音节
jaw	jealous	joint	jolly	j-字母组合
judo	juke-box	June	July	u 在 j 后-开音节
gee	gem	germ	general	e 前 g 读 [dʒ]
gibe	gin	ginger	gist	i 前 g 读 [dʒ]
gybe	gym	gymnasium	gyp	y 前 g 读 [dʒ]
age	cage	gage	large	ge 读 [dʒ]
badge	bridge	edge	fridge	dge 读 [dʒ]
baggage	bandage	garbage	passage	age 读 [dʒ]
education	gradually	graduation	individual	du [dʒu:]
change	exchange	grange	range	_ nge [eindʒ]
messenger	passenger			_ nger [eindʒ]
college				ege 读 [idʒ]

拼音表 (辅音拼元音)（表1）

	[i:]	[i]	[e]	[æ]	[ʌ]	[ə]	[ə:]
[p]	pea	pig	pet	pack	pub	paper	perm
[b]	be	big	bed	bad	bug	number	bird
[t]	tea	tick	test	tap	tub	doctor	turf
[d]	deed	disc	desk	dad	dust	leader	dirt
[k]	keep	kick	kept	kab	kuttern	packer	kerb
[g]	geese	give	get	gap	gum	figure	girl
[f]	feel	fit	fell	fat	fug	forget	fur
[v]	veal	Viz	vest	vac	vulture	liver	virgin
[s]	see	sit	set	sad	such	survey	sir
[z]	zeal	zip	zest	zap	zud	razer	zerk
[θ]	them	thick	theft	thank	thud	method	third
[ð]	these	this	them	that	thus	the	
[ʃ]	sheet	ship	shelf	sham	shut	washer	shirt
[ʒ]	请看辅音拼元音特殊情况的说明						
[r]	read	rib	red	rag	rub	mirror	
[w]	week	will	wet	wax	worry	worker	word
[j]	yeast	Yin	yes	yap	yuck	yahoo	year
[l]	lead	lip	let	lap	luck	ruler	lurk
[m]	meat	miss	met	mad	mud	humour	merge
[n]	need	nit	net	nap	nut	learner	nurse
[ŋ]	请看辅音拼元音特殊情况的说明						
[h]	heat	hit	help	had	hut	habitual	herb
[tr]	treat	trip	trend	track	trust	tradition	
[dr]	dream	drill	dress	drag	drug	dramati	
[ts]	请看辅音拼元音特殊情况的说明						
[dz]	请看辅音拼元音特殊情况的说明						
[tʃ]	cheap	chip	chess	chat	chuck	future	church

| [dʒ] | jeep | jib | jet | jack | just | larger | jerk |

拼音表（辅音拼元音）（表2）

	[ɑ:]	[ɔ]	[ɔ:]	[u]	[u:]	[ei]	[ai]
[p]	park	pot	port	pull	pool	page	pipe
[b]	bard	boss	born	book	boom	bake	bike
[t]	tar	top	torch	took	too	take	time
[d]	dark	dog	dorn	do	doom	date	dime
[k]	kart	kob	kor	cook	kook	Kate	kite
[g]	garb	got	gorge	good	goose	gate	guide
[f]	far	fog	for	foot	fool	face	five
[v]	var	vol	vorte		voom	vane	vice
[s]	sar	sock	sort	soot	soon	same	site
[z]	zarf	zoll	zorse		zoo	zain	zaima
[θ]	tharn	thong	thorn				thigh
[ð]						they	thine
[ʃ]	sharp	shot	short	should	shoot	shape	shy
[ʒ]	请看辅音拼元音特殊情况的说明						
[r]	raft	rock	rorty	rook	room	race	ride
[w]	wamble	wop	warm	wood	wound	wake	wipe
[j]	yard	yob	York	you	yew	Yale	jipe
[l]	lark	lot	lord	look	loop	late	line
[m]	mark	mop	mor	muslin	moon	make	mine
[n]	nark	not	north	nook	noon	name	nine
[ŋ]	请看辅音拼元音特殊情况的说明						
[h]	hard	hop	horn	hook	hoop	hate	hide
[tr]	trance	trot	traum		true	trade	try
[dr]	draft	drop	draw		drew	drake	dry
[ts]	请看辅音拼元音特殊情况的说明						

[dz]	请看辅音拼元音特殊情况的说明					
[tʃ]	chart	chop	chord	choose	chafe	chide
[dʒ]	jar	Job	jor	juice	jade	jive

拼音表（辅音拼元音）（表3）

	[au]	[əu]	[ɔi]	[iə]	[ɛə]	[uə]
[p]	pouch	pole	poise	peony	pair	poor
[b]	bout	bow	boy	bead	bare	boor
[t]	tout	tone	toy	tear	tare	tour
[d]	douse	dope	doyen	dear	dare	dour
[k]	kou	kobe	koine	keir	care	koork
[g]	gouge	go	goiter	gear	gare	gourd
[f]	foul	foe	foil	fear	fare	
[v]	vouch	vote	voice	veer	vary	voorskot
[s]	south	soap	soy	seer		
[z]	zounds	zone	zoid	zero		
[θ]	thou	thole		theory		
[ð]		though			there	
[ʃ]	shout	show		shear	share	sure
[ʒ]	请看辅音拼元音特殊情况的说明					
[r]	rout	role	roister	rear	rare	rural
[w]	wow	woke		weir	wear	
[j]	yowl	yoke	yoick	year	yare	You're
[l]	loud	lone	loyal	clear	lair	lure
[m]	mouth	mode	moist	mere	Mary	moor
[n]	now	note	noise	near		
[ŋ]	请看辅音拼元音特殊情况的说明					
[h]	house	hope	hoist	hear	hare	
[tr]	trout	trope	troika			

[dr]	trought	drome	droit	drear		
[ts]	请看辅音拼元音特殊情况的说明					
[dz]	请看辅音拼元音特殊情况的说明					
[tʃ]	chow	choke	choice	cheers	chair	
[dʒ]	joust	joke	joy			jurist

英语拼音表（辅音拼元音）[特殊情况的说明]

[ʒ]	garage	leisure	luge	pleasure	measure	beige	Jean
	treasure	television		vision			
[ŋ]	sing	length	sang	tongue	long	young	bring
[ts]	eats	pits	pets	cats	cuts	hurts	parts
	lots	sorts	plates	grates	hates		
[dz]	pads	lids	beds	needs	stands	lands	
	spades	grades		blades			

Linan Shi & Shasha Shi

英语拼音练习表 (辅音拼元音)

[p]

pea	pig	pet	pack	pub	paper	perm	park	pot	port
pull	pool	page	pipe	pouch	pole	poise	peony	pair	poor

[b]

be	big	bed	bad	bug	number	bird	bard	boss	born
book	boom	bake	bike	bout	bow		boy	beard	bare	boor

[t]

tea	tick	test	tap	tub	doctor	turf	tar	top	torch
took	too	take	time	tout	tone		toy	tear	tare	tour

[d]

deed	disc	desk	dad	dust	leader	dirt	dark	dog	dorm
do	doom	date	dime	douse	dope	doyen	dear	dare	dour

[k]

keep	kick	kept	cap	cut	packer	kerb	kart	cost	corn
cook	cool	cane	kite	cow	code	coy	care		

[g]

geezer	give	get	gap	gum	younger	girl	garb	got	gorge
good	goose	gate	guide	gouge	go		goiter	gear	gour-met

[f]

feel	fit	fell	fat	fug	forget	fur	far	fog	for
foot	fool	face	five	foul	foe		foil	fear	fare	

[v]

| veal | viz | vest | vac | vulture | liver | virgin | varnish | vomit vortex |
| voo-doo | voo-doo | vane | vice | vouch | vote | voice | veer | vary |

[s]

| see | sit | set | sad | such | survey | sir | sar | sock |
| sort | soot | soon | same | site | south | soap | soy | sear |

[z]

| zeal | zip | zest | zap | zomble | zoo | Zeit-geist | zone zero |

[θ]

| theme | thick | theft | thank | thud | method | third |
| thong | thorn | thigh | thou | thole | theory | |

[ð]

| these | this | them | that | thus | the | they | thine | thou | there |

[ʃ]

| sheet | ship | shelf | sham | shut | washer | shirt | sharp | shot | short |
| should | shoot | shape | shy | shout | show | shear | share | sure | |

[ʒ]

请看英语拼音练习表 (辅音拼元音) [特殊情况的说明]

[r]

| read | rib | red | rag | rub | mirror | raft | rock | rook |
| room | race | ride | rout | roister | role | rare | rear | rural |

[w]

week	will	wet	wax	worry	work	wop	warm
wood	wound	wake	wipe	wow	woke	wear	weir

[j]

yeast	yin	yes	yap	yuck	year	yard	yob
york	you	yew	Yale	yowl	yoke	year	you're

[l]

lead	lip	let	lap	luck	ruler	lurk	lark	lot	lord
look	loop	late	line	loud	lone	loyal	clear	lair	lure

[m]

meat	miss	met	mad	mud	humour	merge	mark	mop	more
Muslin	moon	make	mine	mouth	mode	moist Mary		mere	moor

[n]

need	nit	net	nap	nut	learner	nurse	nark	not
north	nook	noon	name	nine	now	note	noise	near

[ŋ]

请看英语拼音练习表 (辅音拼元音) [特殊情况的说明]

[h]

heat	hit	help	had	hut	habitual	herb	hard	hop	horn
hook	hoop	hate	hide	house	hope	hoist	hare	hear	houri

[tr]

treat	trip	trend	track	trust	tradition	trance	trot
trauma	true	trade	try	trout	trope	troika	

[dr]

| dream | drill | dress | drag | drug | dramatic | draft |
| drop | draw | drew | drake | dry | drought | |

[ts]

请看英语拼音练习表 (辅音拼元音) [特殊情况的说明]

[dz]

请看英语拼音练习表 (辅音拼元音) [特殊情况的说明]

[tʃ]

| cheap | chip | chess | chat | chuck | future | church | chart | chop |
| chord | choose | chafe | chide | chow | choke | choice | cheer | chair |

[dʒ]

| jeep | jib | jet | jack | just | larger | jerk | jar |
| job | juice | jade | jive | joust | joke | joy | jurist |

英语拼音练习表 (辅音拼元音)
[特殊情况的说明]

[ʒ]

beige	garage	luge	leisure	measure
pleasure	treasure	television	vision	

[ŋ]

sing	length	sang	tongue	long	young	length

[ts]

eats	pits	pets	cats	cuts	hurts
parts	lots	sorts	plates	grates	hates

[dz]

needs	lids	beds	pads
blades	grades	spades	

英语元音字母的常用读音规则表

英 语 元 音 字 母	读音规则	例 词		
a 在开音节中读	[ei]	a	take	gate
a 在闭音节中读	[æ]	tap	gas	bad
a 在 R 音节中读	[a:]	bar	far	tar
war 读	[wɔ:]	war	warm	warn
o 在开音节中读	[əu]	go	so	bode
o 在闭音节中读	[ɔ]	box	fox	top
o 在 R 音节中读	[ɔ:]	fork	port	lord
wor 读	[wə:]	word	work	world
u 在开音节中读	[ju:]	puke	tube	duke
u 在闭音节中读	[ʌ]	pub	but	sum
u 在 R 音节中读	[ə:]	fur	burn	turn
e 在开音节中读	[i:]	eve	mete	gene
e 在闭音节中读	[e]	bed	pet	set
e 在 R 音节中读	[ə:]	berg	term	verb
i 在开音节中读	[ai]	I	bike	tide
i 在闭音节中读	[i]	tip	did	sit
i 在 R 音节中读	[ə:]	bird	first	dirt
y 在开音节中读	[ai]	spy	my	sky
		dye	bye	lye
y 在闭音节中读	[i]	gym	myth	nymph
y 作辅音字母时读 [j]	[j]	Yale	yet	york

英语辅音字母的常用读音规则表

英 语 辅 音 字 母	读音规则	例	词	
b 读	[b]	bake	back	bar
		rib	lab.	pub
c 在 e, i, y 前读	[s]	cent	cite	cycle
在 a, o, u 前读	[k]	cake	code	cute
或其它场合读		clock	clinic	bicycle
d 读	[d]	date	did	dark
		sad	bid	hard
		Sydney	mid	seedless
f 读	[f]	face	fit	far
		wife	wolf	leaf
		lift	shaft	helpful
g 在 e, i, y 前读	[dʒ]	germ	gibe	gym
在 a, o, u 前读	[g]	gate	go	gum
或其它场合读		glad	gray	pig
h 读	[h]	hate	hut	hard
j 读	[dʒ]	jade	just	jar
k 读	[k]	kite	kick	kart
		leak	sick	dark
		making	risky	market
l 在单词中	[l]	mill	bill	till
		pile	tile	file
		silk	milk	tilt
在词首读	[l]	late	lot	luck
或元音前读		play	globe	fly
不发音	[ ]	palm	calm	talk
m 在单词中	[m]	slim	sum	mug
		lime	time	same

213

		pump	dump	lamp
在词首读	[m]	make	mist	mark
或元音前读		smoke	smile	smart
n 在单词中	[n]	fan	ten	lantern
		line	fine	pine
		enter	land	fence
在词首读	[n]	name	nap	nark
或元音前读		snake	sneak	snack
p 读	[p]	page	pick	park
		tap	lip	snap
		simple	depth	diploma
q 读	[k]	Iraq		
r 读	[r]	race	red	read
s 在词首读	[s]	stay	sky	smoke
在元音后读	[z]	has	is	was
t 读	[t]	time	tip	tar
		sit	lit	smart
		hottest	potato	plastic
v 读	[v]	vote	vest	verb
		cv	LV	live
		favour	avoid	event
w 读	[w]	wave	wet	week
		swim	sweet	swipe
x 读	[ks]	box	fox	fix
x 在两元音间,重读在后一个元音读	[gz]	example	exam	exact
y 读	[j]	yes	yard	yield
z 读	[z]	zone	zoo	zip
		fuzz	buzz	oz
		buzzard	puzzle	nuzzle

英语26个字母的常用读音规则表

英 语 字 母	读音规则	例		词
a 在开音节中读	[e i]	a	take	gate
a 在闭音节中读	[æ]	tap	gas	bad
a 在 R 音节中读	[a:]	bar	far	tar
war 读	[wɔ:]	war	warm	warn
b 读	[b]	bake	back	bar
		rib	lab.	pub
c 在 e, i, y 前读	[s]	cent	cite	cycle
在 a, o, u 前读	[k]	cake	code	cute
或其它场合读		clock	clinic	bicycle
d 读	[d]	date	did	dark
		sad	bid	hard
		Sydney	mid	seedless
e 在开音节中读	[i:]	eve	mete	gene
e 在闭音节中读	[e]	bed	pet	set
e 在 R 音节中读	[ə:]	berg	term	verb
f 读	[f]	face	fit	far
		wife	wolf	leaf
		lift	shaft	helpful
g 在 e, i, y 前读	[dʒ]	germ	gibe	gym
在 a, o, u 前读	[g]	gate	go	gum
或其它场合读		glad	gray	pig
h 读	[h]	hate	hut	hard
i 在开音节中读	[ai]	I	bike	tide
i 在闭音节中读	[i]	tip	did	sit
i 在 R 音节中读	[ə:]	bird	first	dirt
j 读	[dʒ]	jade	just	jar
k 读	[k]	kite	kick	kart

		leak	sick	dark
		making	risky	market
l 在单词中	[l]	mill	bill	pill
		pile	tile	file
		silk	milk	tilt
在词首读	[l]	late	lot	luck
或元音前读		play	globe	fly
不发音	[ ]	palm	calm	talk
m 在单词中	[m]	slim	sum	mum
		lime	time	same
		pump	dump	lamp
在词首读	[m]	make	mist	mark
或元音前读		smoke	smart	smile
n 在单词中	[n]	fan	ten	lantern
		line	fine	pine
		enter	land	fence
在词首读	[n]	name	nap	nark
或元音前读		Snake	sneak	snack
o 在开音节中读	[əu]	go	so	bode
o 在闭音节中读	[ɔ]	box	fox	top
o 在 R 音节中读	[ɔ:]	fork	port	lord
wor 读	[wə:]	word	work	world
p 读	[p]	page	pick	park
		tap	lip	snap
		simple	depth	diploma
q 读	[k]	Iraq		
r 读	[r]	race	red	read
s 在词首读	[s]	stay	smoke	sky
在元音后读	[z]	has	is	was
t 读	[t]	time	tip	tar

		sit	lit	smart
		hotter	fantastic	potato
u 在开音节中读	[ju:]	puke	tube	duke
u 在闭音节中读	[ʌ]	pub	but	sum
u 在 R 音节中读	[ə:]	fur	burn	turn
v 读	[v]	vote	vest	verb
		cv	LV	live
		favour	avoid	event
w 读	[w]	wave	wet	week
		swim	sweet	swipe
x 读	[ks]	box	fox	fix
x 在两元音间,重读在后一个元音读	[gz]	exact	example	exam
y 在开音节中读	[ai]	spy	my	sky
		dye	bye	lye
y 在闭音节中读	[i]	gym	myth	nymph
y 读	[j]	yes	yard	yield
z 读	[z]	zone	zoo	zip
		fuzz	buzz	oz
		buzzard	puzzle	nuzzle

English Pronunciation for Chinese Speakers

英语元音字母或字母组合的常用读音规则表

元音字母或字母组合	读音规则	例		词
a 在开音节中读	[ei]	a	take	gate
a 在闭音节中读	[æ]	tap	gas	bad
a 在 R 音节中读	[ɑ:]	bar	far	tar
war 读	[wɔ:]	war	warm	warn
a 在 Re 音节中读	[ɛə]	hare	bare	dare
ar + 元音字母读	[ɛər]	vary	wary	variable
air 读	[ɛə]	chair	hair	fair
ai 读	[ei]	aim	pain	rain
ai 读	[e]	said		
ay 读	[ei]	bay	say	pay
ay 读	[e]	says		
aigh 读	[ei]	straight		
au 读	[ɔ:]	August	Autumn	author
all 读	[ɔ:l]	mall	tall	ball
al 读（多数情况）		also	almost	already
al 读（少数情况）	[ɔ:]	talk	chalk	walk
al 读（特殊情况）	[ɑ:]	half	calf	palm
augh 读	[ɔ:]	taught	caught	naught
an 读	[æn]	fan	can	pan
an 读	[ɑ:n]	plant	answer	slant
ance 读	[ɑ:ns]	dance	glance	dance
ass 读	[ɑ:s]	pass	class	glass
aft 读	[ɑ:ft]	after	afternoon	aftermath
ask 读	[ɑ:sk]	ask	flask	mask
asp 读	[ɑ:sp]	rasp	grasp	gasp
ast 读	[ɑ:st]	past	last	fast
air 读	[ɛə]	chair	hair	fair

aw 读	[ɔ:]	law	paw	raw
ange 结尾的单词读	[eindʒ]	change	strange	arrange
a 读(在合成词中)读	[ei]	classmate	mooncake	schoolmate
a 在非重读音节中读	[ə]	ago	about	ahead
ar 在非重读音节中读	[ə]	solar	polar	lunar
age 在非重读音节中读	[i]	passage	village	accurate
ai 在非重读音节中读		curtain	certain	certainly
ay 在非重读音节中读		Sunday	birthday	Friday
ate 在非重读音节中读	[ei]	separate	generate	eliminate
ange 在非重读音节中读		change	strange	orange
a 在非重读音节中读	[æ]		program	diagram
a 在成音节中不发音	[ ]	digital	hospital	principal
o 在开音节中读	[əu]	go	so	bode
o 在闭音节中读	[ɔ]	box	fox	top
o 在 R 音节中读	[ɔ:]	fork	port	lord
wor 读	[wə:]	word	work	world
o 在 Re 音节中读	[ɔ:]	bore	sore	shore
or + 元音字母读	[ɔ:r]	story	glorious	boring
oa 读	[əu]	oak	load	road
oar 读	[ɔ:]	board	boar	soar
oe 读	[əu]	doe	foe	toe
oe 读 (特殊情况)		poem	poet	poetry
ol 读		folk	yolk	folksy
ol 读	[əul]	bolt	bold	volt
old 读	[əuld]	sold	gold	fold
oll 读	[əu]	roll	stroll	toll
on 读	[ɔn]	fond	pond	bond
oor 读 (多数情况)	[ɔ:]	floor	door	Bloor
oor 读 (少数情况)	[uə]	poor	boor	moor
ost 读	[əust]	post	host	most

oul 读	[u]	could	would	should
oun 读	[aun]	round	found	pound
our 读 (多数情况)	[auə]	hour	ours	our
our 读 (少数情况)	[ɔ:]	your	court	four
our 读 (特殊情况)	[uə]	tour	gourd	dour
our 读 (极特殊情况)	[ə:]	journey		
oi 读	[ɔi]	oil	boil	soil
oo (多数情况)	[u:]	fool	too	noon
oo (少数情况)		book	look	took
oo (特殊情况)	[ʌ]	blood	flood	
o 在 m, n, th, v 前读		come	son	nothing
ou 读 (多数情况)	[au]	loud	out	mouth
ou 读 (少数情况)	[ʌ]	cousin	couple	touch
ou 读 (特殊情况)	[u:]	group	you	soup
ou 读 (极特殊情况)	[ɔ]	cough		
ough 读	[ɔ:]	thought	bought	fought
ow 读 (多数情况)	[au]	how	now	cow
ow 读 (少数情况)	[əu]	grow	slow	bow
oy 读	[ɔi]	boy	toy	soy
oon 读	[u:n]	moon	noon	boon
o 在非重读音节中读	[ə]	symbol	produce	correct
or 在非重读音节中读		Tractor	doctor	factor
o 在非重读音节中读	[əu]	potato	also	radio
o 在非重读音节中读	[ɔ]	bookshop	dialogue	workshop
ous 在非重读音节中读	[əs]	famous	nervous	obvious
our 在非重读音节中读	[ə]	labour	colour	neighbour
o 在非重读音节中不发音	[ ]	pardon	button	cotton
u 在开音节中读	[ju:]	puke	tube	duke
u 在闭音节中读	[ʌ]	pub	but	sum
u 在 R 音节中读	[ə:]	fur	burn	turn

u 在 Re 音节中读	[juə]	cure	pure	secure
ur + 元音字母读	[juər]	during	fury	curious
u 读	[u]	put	pull	push
ue 读（多数情况）	[ju:]	due	cue	sue
ue 读（少数情况）	[u:]	glue	blue	true
uy 读	[ai]	buy	guy	
un 读（多数情况）	[ʌn]	fun	bun	sun
un 读（少数情况）	[ʌŋ]	hungry	uncle	punctual
u 在 sh 前, b, f, p 后读	[u]	bush	push	Fush
u 在 j, l, r 后的开音节中	[u:]	June	lunar	rude
u 在 ll 前, b, p 后读	[u]	bull	full	pull
u 在 t 前, p 后读		put	putting	puts
u 在非重读音节中读	[ə]	alb<u>u</u>m	camp<u>u</u>s	s<u>u</u>pport
ur 在非重读音节中读		Auburn		
u 在非重读音节中读	[i]	busy	business	minute
u 在非重读音节中读	[u :]	July	February	century
u 在非重读音节中读	[ju:]	graduate	congratulation	
u 在非重读音节中读	[i]	minute		
u 在非重读音节中不发音	[ ]	buy	build	guess
e 在开音节中读	[i:]	eve	mete	gene
e 在闭音节中读	[e]	bed	pet	set
e 在 R 音节中读	[ə :]	berg	term	verb
e 在 Re 音节中读	[iə]	mere	here	sere
（特殊情况）读	[ɛə]	there	therefore	where
er + 元音字母读	[iər]	serious experience		museum
ea 读（多数情况）	[i:]	sea	tea	pea
ea 读（少数情况）	[e]	head	bread	thread
ea 读（特殊情况）	[ei]	great	steak	break
ee 读	[i:]	see	week	bee
ei 读（多数情况）	[ei]	eight	veil	vein

ei 读 (少数情况)	[i:]	receive	receipt	ceiling
ey 读 (多数情况)	[ei]	they	grey	hey
ey 读 (特殊情况)	[i:]	key		
ear 读 (多数情况)	[iə]	hear	dear	fear
ear 读 (少数情况)	[ɛə]	bear	pear	wear
ear 读 (特殊情况)	[ə:]	learn	earn	earth
eer 读	[iə]	deer	beer	leer
eigh 读 (多数情况)	[ei]	weigh	weight	neighbor
eigh 读 (少数情况)	[ai]	height		
en 读	[e n]	end	ten	hen
ew 读 (多数情况)	[ju:]	pew	mew	dew
ew 读 (少数情况)	[u:]	flew	brew	lewd
ew 读 (特殊情况)	[əu]	sew	lewd	
e 在非重读音节中读	[i]	mark<u>e</u>t	harv<u>e</u>st	r<u>e</u>port
er 在非重读音节中读	[ə]	number	leader	reader
e 在非重读音节中读		college	accident	problem
e 在非重读音节中读	[i:]		maybe	kilometer
ee 在非重读音节中读		coffee	toffee	
ei 在非重读音节中读		surfeit	forfeit	forfeiture
ey 在非重读音节中读		money	donkey	monkey
eer 在非重读音节中读	[iə]	pioneer	engineer	volunteer
ent 在非重读音节中读	[ənt]	student	president	excellent
e 在成音节中不发音	[ ]	recent		
i 在开音节中读	[ai]	I	bi<u>k</u>e	tide
i 在闭音节中读	[i]	tip	did	sit
i 在 R 音节中读	[ə:]	bird	first	dirt
i 在 Re 音节中读	[aiə]	fire	wire	hire
ir + 元音字母读	[aiər]	miry	spiral	siren
ie 读 (多数情况)	[i:]	piece	field	sieve
ie 读 (少数情况)	[ai]	pie	tie	lie

English Pronunciation for Chinese Speakers

ie 读（特殊情况）	[aiə]	diet	piety	
igh 读	[a i]	might	sight	light
ild 读	[aild]	child	mild	wild
in 读	[in]	inch	pin	bin
i 读	[ai]	ninth	sign	
i 读	[i:]	mechine	police	magazine
i 在非重读音节中读	[i]	un*i*t	animal	dustbin
i 在非重读音节中读		notice	practice	favorite
i 在非重读音节中读	[ai]	exercise	realize	satellite
i 在非重读音节中读	[ə]	festival	holiday	possible
i 在合成词中读	[ai]	anytime	sometime	motorbike
ie 在非重读音节中读	[i]	movie	cookie	loonie
iture 在非重读音节中读	[itʃə]	furniture		
ition 在非重读音节中读	[iʃən]	position	preposition	
ision 在非重读音节中读	[iʒən]	division	vision	television
ist 在非重读音节中读	[ist]	scientist	chemist	artist
i 有时不发音	[ ]	pencil	pupil	suit
y 在开音节中读	[ai]	spy	my	sky
		dye	bye	lye
y 在闭音节中读	[i]	gym	myth	nymph
y 作辅音字母时读	[j]	Yale	yet	yarn
y 在非重读音节中读	[i]	bicycle	party	baby

English Pronunciation for Chinese Speakers

英语元音字母或字母组合的常用读音规则表 (特殊情况的说明)

英语元音字母或字母组合	读音规则	例		词
a 读	[e]	many	any	anytime
a 读	[ei]	danger	ranger	stranger
on 读	[ɔn]	fond	pond	bond
on 读 (特殊情况)	[əun]	only		
one 读 (极特殊情况)	[wʌn]	one		
one 读	[ɔn]	gone	shone	
o 读	[u]	woman		
o 读	[i]	women		
o 读	[u:]	move		
o 读		do	to	two
ont 读	[əunt]	don't	won't	
o 读	[əu]	both	loth	clothing
o 读	[u:]	tomb	whom	who
oya 读	[ɔiə]	loyal		
ua 读	[wa:]	suave	guano	
ui 读	[u:]	cruise	bruise	sluice
ui 读	[ju:]	nuisance	suit	
ui 读	[ju:i]	tuition	suicide	suicidal
ui 读	[u:i]	fluid	ruin	
ui 读	[wi]	cuirass	squid	cuisine
ui 读	[i]	build	guild	guitar
ui 读	[ai]	guide	guise	guidance
ui 在非重读音节中读	[i]	circuit		biscuit
ea 读 (多数情况)	[i:]	sea	tea	pea
ea 读 (少数情况)	[e]	head	bread	thread

ea 读（特殊情况）	[ei]	great	steak	break
ea 读（极特殊情况）	[iə]	thertre	real	realtor
eo 读		theory	peon	peony
eir 读（多数情况）	[εə]	their	theirs	heir
eir 读（少数情况）	[iə]	weird	seir	weir
eo 读	[i:]	people		
eu 读（多数情况）	[ju:]	feud	deuce	neuter
ia 读	[aiə]	dial	dialogue	diabetes
ier 读	[iə]	fierce	pier	bier
io 读	[aiə]	pioneer	lion	violin
ia 在非重读音节中读	[iə]	Victoria	Maria	Julia
io 在非重读音节中读		million	union	onion
iu 在非重读音节中读		medium	auditorium	stadium
ier 在非重读音节中读		cashier	premier	frontier

English Pronunciation for Chinese Speakers

英语辅音字母或字母组合的常用读音规则表

英语辅音字母 或字母组合	读音规则	例	词	
b 读	[b]	bake	back	bar
		rib	lab.	pub
bl 读	[bl]	bloom	block	black
br 读	[br]	bring	bright	break
b 在词尾,前有 m 时不发音	[ ]	bomb	lamb	thumb
c 在 e, i, y 前读	[s]	cent	cite	cycle
在 a, o, u 前读	[k]	cake	code	cute
或其它场合读		bicycle	clinic	clock
ch 读（多数情况）	[tʃ]	cheap	chess	chair
ch 读（少数情况）	[ʃ]	champagne	machine	chef
ch 读（特殊情况）	[k]	chemist	Christmas	school
ck 读		back	pack	sick
cl 读	[kl]	clear	cloud	clock
cr 读	[kr]	cry	cream	cross
ciou 读	[ʃə]	delicious		
cial 读	[ʃəl]	special	artificial	social
cian 读	[ʃən]	technician	electrician	musician
在 S s 和 X x 后不发音	[ ]	science	scissors	excited
d 读	[d]	date	did	dark
		sad	bid	hard
		seedless	midnight	Sydney
dr 读	[dr]	dream	drill	dress
ds 在词尾读	[dz]	beds	kids	hands
des 在词尾读		spades	grades	blades
dge 读	[dʒ]	badge	bridge	fridge
f 读	[f]	face	fit	far
		wife	wolf	leaf

		wonderful	shaft	lift
fl 读	[fl]	floor	free	fly
fr 读	[fr]	free	fry	fresh
ful 读	[ful]	wonderful	beautiful	graceful
g 在 e, i, y 前读	[dʒ]	germ	gibe	gym
在 a, o, u 前读	[g]	gate	go	gum
或其它场合读		glad	gray	pig
gn 读	[n]	foreign	campaign	design
gl 读	[gl]	glue	glad	globe
gr 读	[gr]	green	ground	gray
gu 读	[g]	guest	guard	guitar
gu 读	[gw]	languish	anguish	linguist
gue 读	[g]	league	dialogue	fatigue
h 读	[h]	hate	hut	hard
h 在词尾, 不发音	[ ]	Oh	myrrh	Sarah
h 在 ex 和 r 后不发音		exhibition	exhausted	rhyme
j 读	[dʒ]	jade	just	jar
k 读	[k]	kite	kick	kart
		leak	sick	dark
		making	market	risky
k 在词首,后跟 n 时,不发音	[ ]	knife	knee	know
l 在词首读	[l]	late	lot	luck
或元音前读		play	globe	fly
在单词中	[l]	mill	bill	pill
		pile	file	tile
		silk	milk	tilt
不发音	[ ]	palm	calm	talk
land 读	[lənd]	Finland	Scotland	Island
m 在词首读	[m]	make	mist	mark
或元音前读		smoke	smile	smart

在单词中	[m]	pump	dump	lamp
		lime	time	same
		gym	slim	sum
mn 在词尾, n 不发音	[ ]	solemn	column	Autumn
ment 读	[mənt]	payment statement basement		
n 在词首读	[n]	name	nap	nark
或元音前读		snake	sneak	snap
在单词中	[n]	fan	lantern	ten
		fine	line	pine
		enter	land	fence
ng 读	[ŋ]	sang	song	lung
nk 读	[ŋk]	bank	sink	rank
比较级或最高级中的 ng 读	[ŋg]	longer	longest	
ng 后跟 er 读		finger	hunger	anger
ng 后跟 er 读 (特殊情况)	[ŋ]	singer		
ng 后跟 le 读	[ŋgl]	single	mingle	
nge 读	[ndʒ]	change	strange	arrange
p 读	[p]	page	pick	park
		tap	lip	snap
		simple	diploma	depth
ph 读	[f]	phone	phase	graph
pl 读	[pl]	play	plus	plan
pr 读	[pr]	price	proud	pray
q 读	[kju:]	Q	QC	QB
q 读	[k]	Iraq		
qu 读	[kw]	quit	quarter	quite
que 读	[k]	unique	brusque	antique
r 读	[r]	race	red	read
s 在词首读	[s]	stay	smoke	sky
在元音后读	[z]	has	is	was

sh 读	[ʃ]	sheet	ship	shelf
		ash	cash	dish
sc 读	[sk]	scream	screw	scar
sk 读	[sk]	sky	skin	skirt
sp 读	[sp]	spring	spy	speak
st 读	[st]	steel	star	state
str 读	[str]	street	strong	strike
sl 读	[sl]	slope	slow	slim
sm 读	[sm]	smoke	smart	smell
sn 读	[sn]	sneak	sneeze	snap
sq 读	[sk]	squirrel	squeeze	square
sw 读	[sw]	swim	sweep	sweet
stion 读	[stʃən]	question	suggestion	
sion 读	[ʃən]	extension	profession	pension
sion 读	[ʒən]	occasion	decision	collision
sive 读	[siv]	expensive	explosive	passive
sia 读	[ʃə]	Asia	Russia	Asian
sten 读	[sn]	listen	Christen	fasten
stle 读	[sl]	whistle	castle	jostle
sure 读	[ʒə]	measure	pleasure	leisure
t 读	[t]	time	tip	tar
		sit	lit	smart
		hottest	fantastic	potato
th 在实词前读	[θ]	path	north	south
th 在功能词前读	[ð]	this	with	these
tr 读	[tr]	treat	trip	trust
ts 读	[ts]	pets	cats	hats
tes 读		plates	grates	hates
tch 读	[tʃ]	watch	match	patch
tw 读	[tw]	twice	twist	twin

the 读	[ð]	teethe	lathe	bathe
ture 读	[tʃə]	picture	lecture	nature
tion 读	[ʃən]	instruction	education	nation
tory 读	[tri]	factory	victory	
tary 读		Secretary		
tive 读	[tiv]	effective	sensitive	active
tial 读	[ʃəl]	partial	martial	potential
tient 读	[ʃənt]	patient	patience	
ther 读	[ðə]	weather	leather	brother
teen 读	[ti:n]	thirteen	fourteen	fifteen
v 读	[v]	vote	vest	verb
		cv	LV	live
		favour	avoid	event
w 读	[w]	wave	wet	week
		swim	sweet	swipe
w 在 r 前, 不发音	[ ]	wrist	write	wrote
w 在 h 前, h 不发音		where	what	when
wh 在 o 前, w 不发音		whole	who	hour
wa 在闭音节中 读	[wɔ]	wash	watch	want
x 读	[ks]	box	fox	fix
x 在两元音间,重读在后一个元音读	[gz]	example	exact	exam
y 读	[j]	yes	yard	yield
z 读	[z]	zone	zoo	zip
		Fuzz	buzz	oz
		buzzard	puzzle	nuzzle

英语辅音字母或字母组合的常用读音规则表 (特殊情况的说明)

英语辅音字母或字母组合	读音规则	例	词	
g 在 e, i 前读 (特殊情况)	[g]	gear	get	gift
g 在 e 前读 (极特殊情况)	[ʒ]	beige	garage	
gh 读	[f]	cough	enough	laugh
gh 读 (少数情况)	[g]	ghost	ghetto	ghee
m 在辅音字母 n 前, 不发音	[ ]	mnemonic	mnemonics	
p 在词首, 后跟 n 时不发音		pneumonia	pneumatic	
p 在词首, 后跟 s 时不发音		psaltery	psychic	
p 在词首, 后跟 t 时不发音		ptarmigan	pterodactyl	

英语字母或字母组合的常用读音规则表

字 母 或 字 母 组 合	读音	例 词		
a 在开音节中读	[ei]	a	take	gate
a 在闭音节中读	[æ]	tap	gas	bad
a 在 R 音节中读	[ɑ:]	bar	far	tar
war 读	[wɔ:]	war	warm	warn
a 在 Re 音节中读	[ɛə]	hare	bare	dare
ar + 元音字母读	[ɛər]	vary	wary	variable
air 读	[ɛə]	chair	hair	fair
ai 读	[ei]	aim	pain	rain
ai 读	[e]	said		
ay 读	[ei]	bay	say	pay
ay 读	[e]	says		
aigh 读	[ei]	straight		
au 读	[ɔ:]	August	Autumn	author
all 读	[ɔ:l]	mall	tall	ball
al 读 (多数情况)		almost	also	already
al 读 (少数情况)	[ɔ:]	talk	chalk	walk
al 读 (特殊情况)	[ɑ:]	half	calf	palm
augh 读	[ɔ:]	taught	caught	naught
an 读	[æn]	fan	can	pan
an 读	[ɑ:n]	answer	plant	slant
ance 读	[ɑ:ns]	glance	dance	chance
ass 读	[ɑ:s]	pass	class	glass
aft 读	[ɑ:ft]	afternoon	after	aftermath
ask 读	[ɑ:sk]	ask	flask	mask
asp 读	[ɑ:sp]	rasp	grasp	gasp

ast 读	[a:st]	past	last	fast
air 读	[εə]	chair	hair	fair
aw 读	[ɔ:]	law	paw	raw
ange 结尾的单词，读	[eindʒ]	change	strange	arrange
a 读 （在合成词中）	[ei]	classmate		mooncake
a 在非重读音节中读	[ə]	ago	about	ahead
ar 在非重读音节中读		solar	polar	lunar
age 在非重读音节中读	[i]	passage	village	accurate
ai 在非重读音节中读		curtain	certain	certainly
ay 在非重读音节中读		birthday	Sunday	Friday
ate 在非重读音节中读	[ei]	separate		eliminate
ange 在非重读音节中读		change	strange	orange
a 在非重读音节中读	[æ]	diagram		program
a 在成音节中不发音	[ ]	hospital	digital	principal
b 读	[b]	bake	back	bar
		rib	lab.	pub
bl 读	[bl]	bloom	block	black
br 读	[br]	bring	bright	break
b 在词尾，前有 m 时不发音	[ ]	bomb	lamb	thumb
c 在 e, i, y 前读	[s]	cent	cite	cycle
在 a, o, u 前读	[k]	cake	code	cute
或其它场合读	[k]	clock	clinic	bicycle
ch 读 （多数情况）	[tʃ]	cheap	chess	chair
ch 读 （少数情况）	[ʃ]	machine	chef	champagne
ch 读 （特殊情况）	[k]	Christmas	school	chemist
ck 读		back	pack	sick
cl 读	[kl]	clear	cloud	clock
cr 读	[kr]	cry	cream	cross
ciou 读	[ʃə]	delicious		
cial 读	[ʃəl]	artificial	social	special

cian 读	[ʃən]	technician	electrician	
在 S s 和 X x 后不发音	[ ]	science	scissors	excited
d 读	[d]	date	did	dark
		sad	bid	hard
		midnight	seedless	Sydney
dr 读	[dr]	dream	drill	dress
ds 在词尾读	[dz]	beds	kids	hands
des 在词尾读		spades	grades	blades
dge 读	[dʒ]	badge	bridge	fridge
e 在开音节中读	[i:]	eve	mete	gene
e 在闭音节中读	[e]	bed	pet	set
e 在 R 音节中读	[ə:]	berg	term	verb
e 在 Re 音节中读	[iə]	mere	here	sere
(特殊情况) 读	[ɛə]	there	where	therefore
er + 元音字母读	[iər]	serious	period	museum
ea 读 (多数情况)	[i:]	sea	tea	pea
ea 读 (少数情况)	[e]	head	bread	thread
ea 读 (特殊情况)	[ei]	great	steak	break
ee 读	[i:]	see	week	bee
ei 读 (多数情况)	[ei]	eight	veil	vein
ei 读 (少数情况)	[i:]	receive	receipt	ceiling
ey 读 (多数情况)	[ei]	they	grey	hey
ey 读 (特殊情况)	[i:]	key		
ear 读 (多数情况)	[iə]	hear	dear	fear
ear 读 (少数情况)	[ɛə]	bear	pear	wear
ear 读 (特殊情况)	[ə:]	learn	earn	earth
eer 读 (极特殊情况)	[iə]	deer	beer	leer
eigh 读 (多数情况)	[ei]	weigh	weight	neighbor
eigh 读 (少数情况)	[ai]	height		
en 读	[en]	end	ten	hen

ew 读 (多数情况)	[ju:]	pew	mew	dew
ew 读 (少数情况)	[u:]	flew	brew	lewd
ew 读 (特殊情况)	[əu]	sew	lewd	
e 在非重读音节中读	[i]	market	harvest	report
er 在非重读音节中读	[ə]	number	leader	reader
e 在非重读音节中读	[ə]	college	accident	
e 在非重读音节中读	[i:]	maybe	market	kilometer
ee 在非重读音节中读	[i]	coffee	toffee	
ei 在非重读音节中读		forfeit	surfeit	forfeiture
ey 在非重读音节中读		money	donkey	monkey
eer 在非重读音节中读	[iə]	volunteer		engineer
ent 在非重读音节中读	[ənt]	president	student	excellent
e 在成音节中不发音	[ ]	recent		
f 读	[f]	face	fit	far
		wife	wolf	leaf
		wonderful	shaft	lift
fl 读	[fl]	floor	free	fly
fr 读	[fr]	free	fry	fresh
ful 读	[ful]	wonderful	helpful	beautiful
g 在 e, i, y 前读	[dʒ]	germ	gibe	gym
在 a, o, u 前读	[g]	gate	go	gum
或其它场合读		glad	gray	pig
gn 读	[n]	campaign	design	
gl 读	[gl]	glue	glad	globe
gr 读	[gr]	green	gray	ground
gu 读	[g]	guest	guard	guitar
gu 读	[gw]	languish	anguish	linguist
gue 读	[g]	league	dialogue	fatigue
h 读	[h]	hate	hut	hard
h 在词尾, 不发音	[ ]	Oh	myrrh	Sarah

h 在 ex 和 r 后不发音		exhausted	rhyme	
i 在开音节中读	[ai]	I	bike	tide
i 在闭音节中读	[i]	tip	did	sit
i 在 R 音节中读	[ə:]	bird	first	dirt
i 在 Re 音节中读	[aiə]	fire	wire	hire
ir + 元音字母读	[aiər]	miry	spiral	siren
ie 读（多数情况）	[i:]	piece	field	sieve
ie 读（少数情况）	[ai]	pie	tie	lie
ie 读（特殊情况）	[aiə]	diet	piety	
igh 读	[ai]	might	sight	light
ild 读	[aild]	child	mild	wild
in 读	[in]	inch	pin	bin
i 读	[ai]	ninth	sign	
i 读	[i:]	magazine	police	machine
i 在非重读音节中读	[i]	unit	animal	dustbin
i 在非重读音节中读		practice	notice	favorite
i 在非重读音节中读	[ai]	exercise	realize	satellite
i 在非重读音节中读	[ə]	festival	holiday	possible
i 在合成词中读	[ai]	motorbike	anytime	
ie 在非重读音节中读	[i]	movie	cookie	loonie
iture 在非重读音节中读	[itʃə]	furniture		
ition 在非重读音节中读	[iʃən]	preposition	position	
ision 在非重读音节中读	[iʒən]	television	vision	division
ist 在非重读音节中读	[ist]	scientist	chemist	artist
i 有时不发音	[ ]	pencil	pupil	suit
j 读	[dʒ]	jade	just	jar
k 读	[k]	kite	kick	kart
		leak	sick	dark
		making	risky	market
k 在词首后跟 n,不发音	[ ]	knife	knee	know

l 在词首读	[l]	late	luck	lot
或元音前读		play	fly	globe
在单词中读	[l]	mill	bill	pill
		file	tile	pile
		silk	milk	tilt
不发音	[ ]	palm	calm	talk
land 读	[lənd]	Finland	Island	Scotland
m 在词首读	[m]	make	mist	mark
或元音前读		smoke	smile	smart
在单词中读	[m]	pump	dump	lamp
		slim	sum	mum
		time	lime	same
mn 在词尾, n 不发音	[ ]	solemn	column	Autumn
ment 读	[mənt]	payment		statement
n 在词首读	[n]	name	nap	nark
或元音前读		snake	sneak	snap
在单词中读	[n]	enter	land	fence
		fan	ten	lantern
		fine	line	pine
ng 读	[ŋ]	sang	song	lung
nk 读	[ŋk]	bank	sink	rank
比较级或最高级中的 ng 读	[ŋg]	longer	longest	
ng 后跟 er 读		finger	anger	hunger
ng 后跟 er 读 (特殊情况)	[ŋ]	singer		
ng 后跟 le 读	[ŋgl]	single	mingle	pingle
nge 读	[ndʒ]	change	strange	arrange
o 在开音节中读	[əu]	go	so	bode
o 在闭音节中读	[ɔ]	box	fox	top
o 在 R 音节中读	[ɔ:]	fork	port	lord

wor 读	[wə:]	word	work	world
o 在 Re 音节中读	[ɔ:]	bore	sore	shore
or + 元音字母读	[ɔ:r]	story	boring	glorious
oa 读	[əu]	oak	load	road
oar 读	[ɔ:]	board	boar	soar
oe 读	[əu]	doe	foe	toe
oe 读（特殊情况）		poem	poet	poetry
ol 读	[əu]	folk	yolk	folksy
ol 读	[əul]	bolt	bold	volt
old 读	[əuld]	sold	gold	fold
oll 读	[əu]	roll	stroll	toll
on 读	[ɔn]	fond	pond	bond
oor 读（多数情况）	[ɔ:]	floor	door	Bloor
oor 读（少数情况）	[uə]	poor	boor	moor
ost 读	[əust]	post	host	most
oul 读	[u]	could	would	should
oun 读	[aun]	round	found	pound
our 读（多数情况）	[auə]	hour	ours	our
our 读（少数情况）	[ɔ:]	your	court	four
our 读（特殊情况）	[uə]	tour	gourd	dour
our 读（极特殊情况）	[ə:]	journey		
oi 读	[ɔi]	oil	boil	soil
oo（多数情况）	[u:]	fool	too	noon
oo（少数情况）	[u]	book	look	took
oo（特殊情况）	[ʌ]	blood	flood	
o 在 m, n, th, v 前读		come	son	nothing
ou 读（多数情况）	[au]	loud	out	mouth
ou 读（少数情况）	[ʌ]	cousin	couple	touch
ou 读（特殊情况）	[u:]	group	you	soup
ou 读（极特殊情况）	[ɔ]	cough		

ough 读	[ɔ:]	thought	bought	fought
ow 读 (多数情况)	[au]	how	now	cow
ow 读 (少数情况)	[əu]	grow	slow	bow
oy 读	[ɔi]	boy	soy	toy
oon 读	[u:n]	moon	boon	noon
o 在非重读音节中读	[ə]	symbol	produce	correct
or 在非重读音节中读		tractor	doctor	factor
o 在非重读音节中读	[əu]	potato	also	radio
o 在非重读音节中读	[ɔ]	bookshop		dialogue
ous 在非重读音节中读	[əs]	nervous	famous	obvious
our 在非重读音节中读	[ə]	labour	colour	neighbour
o 在非重读音节中不发音	[ ]	pardon	button	cotton
P 读	[p]	page	pick	park
		tap	lip	snap
		simple	depth	diploma
ph 读	[f]	phone	phase	graph
pl 读	[pl]	play	plus	plan
pr 读	[pr]	pray	price	proud
q 读	[kju:]	Q	QC	QB
q 读	[k]	Iraq		
qu 读	[kw]	quit	quarter	quite
que 读	[k]	unique	brusque	antique
r 读	[r]	race	red	read
s 在词首读	[s]	stay	smoke	sky
在元音后读	[z]	has	is	was
sh 读	[ʃ]	sheet	ship	shelf
		ash	cash	dish
sc 读	[sk]	scream	screw	scar
sk 读	[sk]	sky	skin	skirt
sp 读	[sp]	spring	spy	speak

English Pronunciation for Chinese Speakers

st 读	[st]	steel	star	state
str 读	[str]	street	strike	strong
sl 读	[sl]	slope	slow	slim
sm 读	[sm]	smoke	smart	smell
sn 读	[sn]	sneak	snap	sneeze
sq 读	[sk]	square	squeeze	squirrel
sw 读	[sw]	swim	sweep	sweet
stion 读	[stʃən]	question	suggestion	
sion 读	[ʃən]	profession	pension	
sion 读	[ʒən]	occasion	collision	
sive 读	[siv]	expensive	passive	
sia 读	[ʃə]	Asia	Russia	Asian
sten 读	[sn]	listen	Christen	fasten
stle 读	[sl]	whistle	castle	jostle
sure 读	[ʒə]	measure	pleasure	leisure
t 读	[t]	time	tip	tar
		sit	lit	smart
		hottest	fantastic	potato
th 在实词前读	[θ]	path	north	south
th 在功能词前读	[ð]	this	with	these
tr 读	[tr]	treat	trip	trust
ts 读	[ts]	pets	cats	hats
tes 读		plates	grates	hates
tch 读	[tʃ]	watch	match	patch
tw 读	[tw]	twice	twist	twin
the 读	[ð]	teethe	lathe	bathe
ture 读	[tʃə]	picture	nature	lecture
tion 读	[ʃən]	instruction	nation	education
tory 读	[tri]	factory	victory	
tary 读		secretary		

tive 读	[tiv]	effective	sensitive	active
tial 读	[ʃəl]	partial	martial	potentil
tient 读	[ʃənt]	patient	patience	
ther 读	[ðə]	weather	leather	brother
teen 读	[ti:n]	thirteen	fourteen	fifteen
u 在开音节中读	[ju:]	puke	tube	duke
u 在闭音节中读	[ʌ]	pub	but	sum
u 在 R 音节中读	[ə:]	fur	burn	turn
u 在 Re 音节中读	[juə]	cure	pure	secure
ur + 元音字母读	[juər]	during	fury	curious
u 读	[u]	put	pull	push
ue 读（多数情况）	[ju:]	due	cue	sue
ue 读（少数情况）	[u:]	glue	blue	true
uy 读	[ai]	buy	guy	
un 读（多数情况）	[ʌn]	fun	bun	sun
un 读（少数情况）	[ʌŋ]	hungry	uncle	punctual
u 在 sh 前, b, f, p 后读	[u]	bush	push	Fush
u 在 j, l, r 后开音节词中读	[u:]	June	lunar	rude
u 在 ll 前, b, p 后读	[u]	bull	full	pull
u 在 t 前, p 后读		Put		
u 在非重读音节中读	[ə]	alb<u>u</u>m	camp<u>u</u>s	s<u>u</u>pport
ur 在非重读音节中读		Auburn		
u 在非重读音节中读	[i]	business	busy	minute
u 在非重读音节中读	[u :]	February	July	century
u 在非重读音节中读	[ju:]	continue	congratulation	
u 在非重读音节中读	[i]	minute		
u 在非重读音节中不发音	[ ]	buy	build	guess
v 读	[v]	vote	vest	verb
		cv	LV	live

		favour	avoid	event
w 读	[w]	wave	wet	week
		swim	sweet	swipe
x 读	[ks]	box	fox	fix
x 在两元音间,重读在后一个元音读	[gz]	example	exact	exam
y 读	[j]	yes	yard	yield
y 在开音节中读	[ai]	spy	my	sky
		dye	bye	lye
y 在闭音节中读	[i]	gym	myth	nymph
y 作辅音字母时读	[j]	Yale	yet	yarn
y 在非重读音节中读	[i]	bicycle	party	baby
z 读	[z]	zone	zoo	zip
		fuzz	buzz	oz
		buzzard	puzzle	nuzzle

英语字母或字母组合的常用读音规则表 (特殊情况的说明)

英 语 字 母 或 字 母 组 合	读音规则	例	词	
a 读	[e]	anyone	any	many
a 读	[ei]	danger	ranger	grange
on 读	[ɔn]	fond	pond	bond
on 读 (特殊情况)	[əun]	only		
one 读 (极特殊情况)	[wʌn]	one		
one 读	[ɔn]	gone	shone	
o 读	[u]	woman		
o 读	[i]	women		
o 读	[u:]	move		
o 读		do	to	two
ont 读	[əunt]	don't	won't	
o 读	[əu]	both	loth	clothes
o 读	[u:]	tomb	whom	who
oya 读	[ɔiə]	loyal		
ua 读	[wa:]	suave	guano	
ui 读	[u:]	cruise	bruise	sluice
ui 读	[ju:]	suit		
ui 读	[ju:i]	tuition	suicide	suicidal
ui 读	[u:i]	fluid	ruin	
ui 读	[wi]	cuirass	squid	cuisine
ui 读	[i]	build	guild	guitar
ui 读	[ai]	guide	guise	guidance
ui 在非重读音节中读	[i]	circuit	biscuit	
ea 读 (多数情况)	[i:]	sea	tea	pea
ea 读 (少数情况)	[e]	head	bread	thread
ea 读 (特殊情况)	[ei]	great	steak	break
ea 读 (极特殊情况)	[iə]	theatre	real	realtor

eo 读		theory	peony	peon
eir 读 (多数情况)	[εə]	their	theirs	heir
eir 读 (少数情况)	[iə]	weird	weir	seir
eo 读	[i:]		people	
eu 读 (多数情况)	[ju:]	neuter	deuce	feud
ia 读 pneumatic	[aiə]	dial	dialogue	diabetes
ier 读	[iə]	fierce	pier	bier
io 读	[aiə]	lion	pioneer	violin
ia 在非重读音节中读	[iə]	Julia	Victoria	Maria
io 在非重读音节中读		union	million	onion
iu 在非重读音节中读		medium	auditorium	
ier 在非重读音节中读		cashier	premier	frontier
g 在 e, i 前读 (特殊情况)	[g]	gear	get	gift
g 在 e 前读 (极特殊情况)	[ʒ]	beige	garage	
gh 读	[f]	cough	enough	laugh
gh 读 (少数情况)	[g]	ghost	ghetto	ghee
m 在辅音字母 n 前, 不发音	[ ]	mnemonic	mnemonics	
P p 在词首, 后跟 N n 时不发音		pneumatic	pneumonia	
P p 在词首, 后跟 S s 时不发音		psaltery	psychic	
P p 在词首, 后跟 T t 时不发音		ptarmigan	pterodactyl	